From
Out of the
Sand

From
Out of the
Sand

STEVE SIETING

CITI OF BOOKS

CITIOFBOOKS, INC.
3736 Eubank NE Suite A1
Albuquerque, NM 87111-3579
www.citiofbooks.com
Hotline: 1 (877) 389-2759
Fax: 1 (505) 930-7244

Ordering Information:
Quantity sales. Special discounts are available on quantity purchases by corporations, associations, and others. For details, contact the publisher at the address above.

Printed in the United States of America.

| ISBN-13: | Softcover | 979-8-89391-475-7 |
| | eBook | 979-8-89391-476-4 |

Library of Congress Control Number: 2024925193

Table of Contents

Poems by Eleanor Sieting

Poems by Steven M. Sieting II

My Foot Prints Though Life

ACKNOWLEDGEMENTS

I thank my mother and father. I never doubted they loved me, because their eyes said it every day. We were poor in finances but not in spirit. They encouraged us to be the best we could be and loved us for who we were. When we failed, they helped us pick up the pieces and get going again. I enjoyed my youth in large part due to my parents' love, support, faith, and trust that they placed on my life. I can't imagine growing up any happier, even though I was an introverted child. My parents have always been simple people who led a simple life and made the very best of it every step of the way. I love them dearly.

I thank my wife, Lynn, for supporting my writing. Lynn never balked at the thought of me writing a book and has supported me in every phase of the process. She has listened to me and offered her much needed suggestions and corrections.

As I began writing, I started to share my faith at work with some of my coworkers. Jonathan Sanders, known as Gabe, and I shared an office. He and I worked very well together, and we became good friends, sharing family stories and laughing at each other's problems and family issues. Unlike most people, Gabe did not just read my poetry and leave it at that. He knew me and accepted me for who I am, and he politely offered suggestions to encourage me. I am so grateful for his honesty and support, but most of all for his friendship. He never did say I was bad, and we had a few laughs at a few of my poems, so I kept sending him most of my work for review.

I also thank my mother-in-law, Yvonne Black. She is the biggest fan of my poetry. Her interest encouraged me when I allowed few people to see my poems.

My close friends, Stephen and Rita Hoy, who helped me with this book, and Keith and Kathy Trout are good friends who have always encouraged and lifted Lynn and me in prayer. I am so thankful to have them as true friends.

My Pastor, Mark Merrill, at the Assembly in Warner Robins, Georgia, is always ready to listen kindly to my words and encourage me. Since he arrived at our church, his teaching has given me strength in my lowest times. Before he arrived, I was at the point of quitting church altogether. His ear was mine without judgment, and even though I did not confess things to him, he knew in his heart the state of my spiritual condition. His love for and acceptance of me was freely given, and for that, I thank him.

INTRODUCTION

At the Georgia Men's Advance Retreat weekend in 2010, I felt led by the Holy Spirit to write a book. I consider myself the last person qualified to do so, but in obedience, I began the journey to this end. The burden never left me, and I started writing poetry, not knowing what I would write or where the words would come from. I discovered that when I put the pencil to paper apart from the world, I found something that I never dreamed of finding. My eyes became open to who I am in the Lord, and in doing so, I came to know the Holy Spirit within me. I also learned I can trust Him as I take each step, even when I do not understand the complete picture. This can only occur through obeying God's Word, praying, and following His Spirit.

It is by obedience that this very private person is being called out of his comfort zone into the open to let you know you are not alone. You can overcome. We all have obstacles, and we all have excuses. Really listen to your own words to see if excuses are holding you hostage from becoming an overcomer in your own life through Christ. He has helped me come from an uneducated, inward person to be respected in my area of work. While most people know I can't spell very well, they don't know I had a very low reading level when I graduated high school. Only those close to me know I had problems keeping my eyes and mind focused. God has led me out of my comfort zone that was my sand play area as a child and placed me in positions where I could grow. It was not always pretty when I got my hands on some of the tasks, but He can make all things work to our good when we follow His leading.

My self-observation came from a desire to do better in many areas of my life. It helped me overcome shyness and my low reading skills. I found the Holy Spirit and prayer are the keys that enabled me to be accountable to the Lord. And in return, He lifts me as I follow His lead. It was this same seeking and hearing from the Holy Spirit that caused me to face my sinful state and has led to spiritual growth. Many of my poems are confessions from my heart about the condition I have walked through. I am well aware many people have overcome much harder things and lived through more difficult times, but the need to overcome is the same.

It is my hope that through sharing my feelings and failures, you will be encouraged and strengthened and in so doing, help you seek private time with the Holy Spirit to improve your spiritual walk with the Lord.

This book contains poetry from three generations of my family. Hopefully, you will find pleasure in the heartfelt words, and they will make you stop and reflect about your personal relationships with your family and the Lord. The poetry in this book is by my mother, Eleanor Sieting; my son, Steven Sieting II, and me. It is through life's experiences that the heart sings its songs. They are the songs of joy and of despair. There are other songs I felt led by the Lord to write and share with others. I hope you will feel encouraged to find you're not alone. We need to learn to reject judgment by ourselves as well as from others. Overcoming the barriers we have will help lead us to our rightful place at the foot of the Savior. Although I am far from perfect, like Paul, it is my heart to say, "Follow me as I follow Christ." Each of us has but one life to live, and it should be lived like a song with a sweet melody and words of life that matter.

The poetry has been placed in the order that I completed them to chronicle my spiritual journey.

Poems by
Steven Sieting

The Lord Is My Shepherd

The Lord is my Shepherd, my guiding light. In His grace my soul delights. Read His Word, so straight and true. Live His Word; it will carry you through. The path He made is still in sight. Just follow Jesus; the path is bright.

Christ Jesus always was and always will be. Give Him your life; it's simple you see. After you do comes the real test, but in your trials, He'll be manifest. For this is when you learn and grow in how to let God's love to show. For in each of us His light should shine, not just a little but all of the time.

Reference: Psalm 23

I think that it is fitting that the Lord had me write this poem first. I talk about living life in accordance with the 23 Psalm in the section of Cancer and after hearing from the Lord. I refer to it as living life as a "No-Matter-What" Disciple of Jesus. It's about totally trusting Jesus, His word, and obeying them because they are life to our soul.

Sacrifice

Sacrifice, oh sacrifice.
What is within you, oh sacrifice?
A change of lifestyle, need, or want.
To pay the price for something you want.
Or to find His strength, power, and will.
Then go forth without doubt or self-will.

The Bible tries to show your way
To put on righteousness in Jesus, His way.
Through parables, faith, and deeds
Manifested by Jesus's life you were indeed.
Into my life, make yourself at home
Until my Lord Jesus calls me home.
Steve Sieting
Reference: Luke 14:27

Lynn and I were married in front of the fireplace in her parents' home. Few people were in town, since we got married on a church softball tournament weekend. Lynn and I left shortly after the wedding. I only had two nights before I had to return to my submarine, because we were going out on a South American run for ten weeks.

Our Path to Date

When we first met, we laughed all day.
Our first date was at San Francisco Bay.
We walked the beach, so cool and breezy.
The time went fast; the steps were easy.

In the navy, my boat went to sea.
As a sailor, I asked you to marry me.
Your dad questioned the choice of me for you.
He kept silent and saw it through.

The keys of the piano were pressed down.
The "Wedding March" began to sound.
"I'm scared and cannot move," I heard you say.
"Take the first step, woman," I replied that day.

Time has marched on; I still love your laugh.
Twenty-six years later, it's been a good path.
Loving you has been nice and breezy.
The time has been fast, and the steps have been easy.

Your loving husband,
Steve
(Christmas 2006)

An ending has a way of making you think about the beginning and the journey that brought you to the very place you stand. At the hospice center north of Zephyrhills, Florida, I leaned over my mother's bed to kiss her and tell her good-bye for the last time. We knew she would die soon. I placed my hand on her cheek and caressed it to connect with her somehow. She was unresponsive at this point, but I needed that one last touch. For me, it was a way of telling her I loved her. I also told her we knew it was time for her to pass, that it was all right, and that she would be missed. As I drove back to my home and family in Georgia, I cried because I missed her. I wondered if I should have stayed with my father and brother, Gordon, until she passed. It was soon after her passing that I wrote a poem in her memory, "Our Last Good-Bye," to help me deal with my feelings. It was after my mother's death most of my poetry writing has occurred.

Our Last Good-Bye

Stroking your hair and caressing your cheek.
I can't help; I only weep.
I know you love me with all of your heart.
Your love for me was from the start.
Before I give you my last hug and kiss,
I want you to know you'll truly be missed.
I am thankful for your words, guidance, and love.
I know now they came from above.
You taught me to judge right from wrong,
And your prayers were for me, all the day long.
You cheered me on and shared my tears.
Our time together has turned into years.
I'm so grateful, more than most.
That's my mom, I'll always boast.
You tatted and sown and carried your cross.
You're now gone; it's our great loss.
Missing you always, memories I see.
Every memory lets me know you're a part of me.
Thank you, Mom.
Love,
Steve
(March 2010)

My mother about the time my father retired

Many people in the area know Lynn. She has always been outgoing and funny, and because she has worked in the school system, we seldom go anywhere we don't stop to talk with someone. I have a great deal of respect for my bride, Lynn. She has earned it and I trust her implicitly. I have faith my privacy will remain with her. I have full confidence that she does not talk poorly about me when I am not in her presence. She knows I am not perfect, and she loves me completely. I trust her with my heart, fears, and secrets, and I know they will remain with her. While she may not be perfect, she is for me. I love her more today than I ever have.

Love is essential for a good marriage, and yet I found there can be more that will enrich your feelings for your spouse without any action on their part. I call it honoring my mate. One way I honor Lynn, is when I perform tasks that she would normally do, I do them with her in mind. I give thanks for her and lift her up while I'm working in her place. I do the work cheerfully. It makes me feel like I am giving her a gift of love, because I put my heart—along with my effort—into action. The effort I give in these times is the best I have, as if it really matters. It is with this type of attitude that I wrote the poem "I Still Like You! I Still Love You!" I found you have to be forgiving when you honor someone, because like the last line in the poem, "each day is followed by another."

Lynn and I also honor each other every day before I leave the house for work. The last thing we do is hold each other and pray together. It brings us closer together mentally and spiritually. We really enjoy these heartfelt moments together. Lynn works with young children, so I make sure she gets the first portion of my time when I get home so she can talk and release her burdens of the day. I realize her need to be expressive in ways I am not. By giving her time to do so, I show her I care for her feelings and needs.

I Still Like You! I Still Love You!

We were each alone; I was so different from you.
Together so playful, laughter we knew.
Eyes showed bright with each passing glance.
Our love grew with each advance.

Vows given; vows received.
United as one, we believed.
Flesh of my flesh, and bone of my bone,
Seldom apart, together we've grown.

Nurturing children going to and fro.
How time passed; where did it go?
Children departed to journey alone.
Hope they enjoy life and make a home.

Questions arise, how did marriage last?
What's your secret? What's your past?
Simply live life, and try not to boast.
Love and respect, make God the host.

Life, like waves, will change with the tides.
Have faith in your mate, and keep them at your side.
Choose standards beforehand of what you might face.
If you don't, you're sure to give chase.

Work together and honor your mate.
Say you're sorry; it's never too late.
Share your dreams, and dream of each other.
Know each day is followed by another.
Steve Sieting
(June 2010)

Daddy

Daddy worked hard, much like a slave.
Simple in life, simply he gave.
No complaints, so little pay.
He did it for us, day after day.
Money was tight, but he made it last.
We were poor, yet we had a blast.
Daddy never said much, but we knew every look.
Each glance our way, read like a book.
Daddy took care of our simple mother.
He loved and respected her like no other.
I come to love Daddy's simple quiet way.
That is why I love simple and quiet today.
Daddy, I Love you,
Steve
(July 16, 2010)

Dad is a very quiet man.
This picture was taken about the time of his retirement.

With Me Every Step, Every Day

On life's road I did roam.
I was proud to be on my own.
Until I met one so pure and true,
My sin revealed and then I knew.
All I did was all for not.
So, in Jesus I cast my lot.
Now a sinner saved by grace,
Not one sin can I erase.
I found the Savior who died for me.
Jesus Christ paid my penalty.
With Jesus I am never alone.
He is my precious cornerstone.
Though storms and winds blow my way,
I pray to Him my soul will stay.
Holy Spirit, reside in me
Light my path; let me see.
Let me hear Your still small voice.
I want Your will to be my choice.
It's Your love that drew me in,
In from a life, I now call sin.
It's not always easy to carry the cross.
But if I don't, others will be lost.
Knowing You're with me every step, every day,
Leads me onward to heaven and Your way.
Steve Sieting
(July 2010)

I went through a long period in my life when I was under attack by someone seeking to profit in any way possible. (I will go into more detail at the end of the book.) When you feel threatened, it is easy to retaliate and operate in the flesh. I did not want to do this. I looked for Scriptures where God fought the battles for His children and took them as my own to find peace amid my storm and for guidance. This poem was my prayer during that period of my life. (Reference: Exodus 14:14, Deuteronomy 1:29-30 and Jude 1:24-24)

Go before Me Lord, This I Pray

Wicked in ways, the deceiver prays.
Luring temptations he brings my way.
Distractions he provides to further my stray.
He knows my weaknesses and sees my ways.
I know I am not in this fight alone.
The Comforter is here to guide me home.
If I am to follow, then You must lead.
Give me Your ear, Lord, this I plead.
Go before me, Lord, this I pray.
Fight my battles, light my way.
For You know the ways of the Enemy.
You know the trials that are before me.
Show me the snares and the wages of sin.
Grant me Your power, Your word within.
Go before me, Lord, this I pray.
Fight my battles, light my way.
Steve Sieting
(July 28, 2010)
Reference: Deuteronomy 31:8

The Drowning

My first grandson, Tyler, has had a special place in my heart even before he was born, because I knew he would never really know what having a true father was about. I did my best to be that father figure for him. It was best my daughter did not marry the father, because he was always in trouble and was very abusive toward her. One day I was on my knees pulling a few weeds growing between the wall and the pool walkway. Tyler was about two and a half years old, and came up to me wearing his bib overalls. I told him, "Hi," smiled, and turned back to finish my task. Tyler must have gone right to the pool ladder and climbed down into the pool. Mind you, I was not four feet away, and he never made a sound. When I turned around, he was gone from sight. As I stood, I saw him underwater, his arms out to the side, like he was on the cross. His eyes were wide open and staring upward. The pool jet pressure was slowly pushing him out to the deep end of the pool. I will never forget the look of him underwater. I quickly snatched him out with one hand on the bib overalls, and he started breathing immediately.

I told you this story because I was drowning in depression, failing too often to pray and read the Bible. This made me feel so isolated at church. All the words sounded like someone talking through water. The message could not get through, and I felt untouchable. The church had rented the movie theater to see *The Passion of the Christ*, and to be honest, I was cold as a stone and unmoved. I did pray some, and God answered most of the few I prayed. Yet I could not get back, because I knew I had failed and felt so dirty. I could not get to the feeling and knowledge that I was forgiven and remained depressed and isolated.

As time passed, I finally got to the point I heard Satan in my spirit during a Wednesday night service tell me, "Your religion does not work." The church was in search of a new pastor, and I had made up my mind that if he did not work out, I was done with the act and quitting church for good. At another Wednesday night service, Sister Etah Garcia was speaking, and I knew it was for me. It spoke to my naval sense about not jumping from the ship and to hold on.

When the new pastor arrived, I was still suffering. I said a prayer when I was alone in my chair. I became silent and then I heard the Spirit say to me "I hear your cry." He then brought to my mind the image of my grandson in the pool and how he looked. I knew I was no different in my drowning in depression, hoping for somebody to snatch me up so I could breathe and hear again. The pressure of life was pushing me away, and I was in silence at church and at home, slowly heading out to the world. Hearing the Holy Spirit say He heard my cry was the pulling me up from drowning that I had longed for. I needed to be rescued.

It was consistency that God wanted out of me, because I was not dependent on His sufficiency. The poem "He Heard My Cry" is also about my journey back to the Lord, walking through hard times and darkness. It is how God took my consistency in the way I lived life and used it to break me, so I would no longer be proud of myself but depend on Him.

How many people are drowning inside the church, unable to hear the message because they have sinned or they can't make the connection? They are underwater, with life's current pushing them out the church doors. And they never make a sound. They have spiritually drowned right in front of us, and they leave the church feeling like there is no hope for them. I can only tell you what it feels like. We, the church body, need to make sure we make a connection, so people can be rescued within the church's doors. They need to know the Lord hears their cry as well.

"I heard your cry." That was all He said, but I can't tell you what that has done for me. To know He has spoken to rescue me and that I do have His ear is very dear to me. I know I will never be alone again, and it is more than enough!

My buddy Tyler and me about the time of his near drowning.

Psalm 40:1 says, "I waited patiently for the Lord; he inclined to me and heard my cry.

He Heard My Cry

Taught from my youth to do my best.
That's what was expected, it was my test.
I learned to please others by what was done.
Praises received was part of the fun.
Introduced to Jesus, His works and His way.
I made a decision to follow Him that day.
As I was taught, I gave Him my all.
I worked hard and tried not to fall.
Offerings and sacrifices I freely gave,
All the while wondering if I was saved.
Proud of my service, yet I felt so alone.
Do you even notice me from Your great throne?
Asking for blessings, your smile my way.
I need to hear from You; I hope it's today.
Working for you right from the start,
I always felt that I did my part.
Finally, I was broken in spirit, contrite in heart.
I cried out to Jesus, where do I start?
Realizing all I did was all for not.
My pride was now gone, and my life in knots.
Hearing my cry, He held me close.
That's really what I needed the most.
He spoke life into my heart, and that's when I knew
He wanted me, and not what I could do.
Steve Sieting
(October 28, 2010)
Reference: Psalm 34:17

He's All I Want

My Lord loves; He's all I want.
He loved me first, when I was still filled with sin.
So much so, I had to let Him in.
My Lord is caring; He's all I want.
He knows me personally and touches my soul.
So much so, he made me whole.
My Lord is Holy; He's all I want.
His word is light and is always true.
So much so, they can prevail in you.
My Lord is alive; He's all I want.
He arose from the dead and is alive today.
So much so, He is the only way.
My Lord is with me; He's all I want.
Though times get rough, He'll be with me through each test.
So much so, He'll carry me when I need a rest.
My Lord is forgiving; He's all I want.
Knowing the condition I'm in, He calls out to me.
So much so, when I pray, He sets me free.
(November 28, 2010)
Reference :2 Corinthians 9:8-11

From my struggles in the navy to my deepest depression that lasted ten years in silence, I learned God purposely placed me in some of the circumstances so He could walk me through them. The list goes on and on of how God does not move the mountains in our lives so that we might learn and grow in Him. Having walked through the mountain passes and down the trail onto the flatland, I can look at the awesome view of His abundant grace and mercy, which guided me even when I was unwilling to follow. The path he chose for me has convinced me that conversion is as daily need as I grow in His grace. This is what the poem "Mountains" means to me.

Mountains

You can fuss and fume; this journey is hard.
Everyday problems often loom large.
Molehills in the distance turn to mountains at hand.
I often wish I knew the lay of the land.
Prayers raised in faith for mountains to move,
More often than not, the mountains refused.
With choices to make, my prayers turned to searching,
And that's when I would find an old narrow path, and how it did wind.
As the path breaks into the clearing and the mountains turn into a view,
I now realize the path was God's way, and He saw me through.
By searching the pathway, I listened and grew.
I now know that if the journey had been easy and the land nice and flat,
I would have never searched or raised a prayer.
I would never know Jesus, my cross He did bare.
Rejoicing is mine, and I hear His words.
The mountains are my testimony, and I am in awe of the view.
Choose you this day, who will you serve?
As for me and my house, we will serve the Lord!
Praise Him from whom all blessings come.
Steve Sieting
(December 4, 2010)
Reference: Proverbs 16:9,
Psalms 32:8, and Proverbs 3:5,6

My parents had eyes that said it all to us kids. My daddy did not have to ask for things at the dinner table. We would see him looking and knew instinctively what he wanted, and we would pass it to him.

They Were More than a Parent

We knew what they would say, and we'd call anyway.
Each look had a meaning, and each look was well known.
And only heaven could help you when you got home.
Those times are past, and we reminisce.
Stories expand with each point of view.
One thing is certain; they bring a laugh or two.
Recited many times, they never grow old.
Yet from their lips, there are no more stories to be told.
For when they pass, we're much more than sad.
They weren't just a parent; they were Mom and Dad.
There is a void that will never be filled.
I've adopted their teaching and many of their ways.
Many memories I keep, yet some fade away.
One thing I know that will never subside.
They are the feelings I have for them deep inside.
I am thankful and grateful for their love through the years.
Steve Sieting
(December 5, 2010)

The poem "Drip" is about how it feels to slowly run out of living water without any source to replace it. I had gone for a long time without reading the Bible and praying. At the end of this period, I found nothing but dry bones and an empty, cracked shell. This was my way of expressing emptiness in my spirit, where there was once a container filled with water. The poem "Sealed" is also about this time of my life and was meant to be part of "Drip," but I just could not make them work together. I can honestly say I was depressed for this entire ten-year period of my life. Most people never knew, because it is not my nature to complain. I was taught to do my best no matter what, and that's what I did through consistency in living life.

Drip

D-r-i-p
D-r-i—p
D-r-i—p
Water will flow
As long as it has a source and a place to go.

Drip
Drip
Drip
The rate will increase.
Erosion occurs, the source depletes.

D-r-i-p
D-r-i-p
D-r—r
The source is gone.
Where it flowed, no one knows.
Steve Sieting
(July 16, 2011)

Sealed

Life worn, sin torn, my faith flowed away.
I failed to yield, I failed to pray
For the Lord to seal this jar of clay.
Nor did I pause to read His letter,
To quench my thirst and to know Him better.
Cracks in my clay appeared, water began to flow.
Little by little, where did it go?
Lost and alone, empty as could be.
I returned to the source, the one who died for me.
He sealed my heart, cleansed me of sin.
A fountain now flows, He placed within.
Where there were once only drops, a river begins.
With a source so abundant, I now overflow.
Spilling out for Him, He knows where it goes.
Steve Sieting
(July 16, 2011)
Reference: Jeremiah 31:25

Our family regularly attended church weekly. The church would have social events such as banquets, wedding parties, and so forth. They used real plates and silverware, which meant someone had to wash the dishes. This suited my father more than dressing up and attending the social event. His choice to serve the church in this capacity automatically enlisted the assistance of his four sons, and my lot was cast.

When I got the chance, I'd peak my head around the corner to see what was going on. I wanted so badly to be a part of the dinner party. Well, being only about six years old, I did not ask why we were the family that always had kitchen duty, but I drew my own conclusion as to why we could not attend the dinner. I assumed it was because we were poor, and our family just did not measure up to the rest of the congregation standards. This affected me for many years. It caused some relationships to fail, because I assumed I was not up to what others should be accustomed to. If I thought a girl's family had money, I did not ask her out. If I did start liking someone and she liked me, the relationship did not last long, because I could not make it work. Relationships were often doomed from the beginning. I just knew I was not good enough for them. I did have one relationship that lasted through high school and beyond, but it was a distant relationship that was encouraged by her parents. They liked me and were very supportive of the relationship and treated me like I was their son. I did not realize I had built a wall in my mind as a child that lasted until after I entered the navy. This early childhood event and assumption that dominated my life for so long is what the poem "Walls" is about.

I wish that childhood assumption was the only wall I ever built, but since I keep things inside, there are sometimes epic battles going on in my mind. I seldom share my feelings, so no one knows what I was—and am—suffering. It's a tough way to live, and it's a miracle our family has survived. I am getting better at expressing myself. I find it hard to confront the very words that come out of my mouth, because once they are out, you can't take them back. You must face them and their consequences.

Today, I think about the various dinner parties I wanted to attend when I read in the Bible that God invited us all to come and dine at His marriage supper. Yet few make their way to attend. If they really had an understanding of the importance of the invitation, and how it affects their eternal future, I would hope things would be different. We seem to be running a race but don't have a clue as to what the real prize is at the finish line.

In the bible, the people that were invited gave a good excuse as to why they couldn't come to the celebration dinner. While an excuse in itself may not be a sin, yet it is sin when we self-justify our ways and fail to commit to the Lord. We make our excuses and go about our way thinking that we've escaped only fooling ourselves into failing to repent of our ways. I've heard the old saying many times "that the road to hell is paved with good intentions!" All are invited. It is up to each of us to answer His invitation. Reference: Matthew: 22 1-14

Walls

Nothing solved, nothing gained.
A place to go, a place of pain.
Each one is different, yet the same.
A place to go, others we blame.
To escape, make an excuse, or lie.
Feelings are deep, feelings we hide.
Inner thoughts, we take our leave.
Inner thoughts, ourselves deceive.
Justifying feelings by what we meant.
Condemning others for the message they sent.
Assumptions are many in thoughts all alone.
Each one seems right, yet none build a home.
A wall that is built, real or perceived,
Is a wall nonetheless to those who believe.
No matter their height, they limit the view.
They only stop us from the things we should do.
To overcome these walls of division,
Each builder must make a decision.
It is certain each wall must come down
If we care and want love to abound.
With gentle mercy each block will surrender.
Withdrawn no more, your regard will be tender.
Steve Sieting
(July 24, 2011)
Reference Proverbs 18:1

A young lady in the church choir spoke in tongues and the message started out with the words "I still call". I felt impressed in my spirit that the message had to be heard more than once. These are the words I felt led to write in the coming days.

I Still Call

I still call; do you know My voice?
My words are clear; you have a choice.
I have time for all who believe.
Weary and burdened come unto to Me.

I still call; do you know My plan?
Freely it's given; you should know who I Am.
My words are life; My Son I gave.
Know Him as Lord, He came to save.

I still call; do you know My names?
Each has a purpose; I am one in the same.
I know your needs and can meet each one.
Trust and believe in Me; the battle is won.

I still call; My peace is your rest.
Place your hope in Me, and I will bless.
Your faith I gave; seek Me, and you'll find
Grace and mercy; they are divine.

I still call; I wait for My bride.
I am coming for her to bring by My side.
Ready yourself. Do not delay,
For no one knows the hour or the day.

When I call, there's no measure of man.
No one will see that I am the great I Am.
A void will be left, the world on its own,
Raging destruction, the saved will be home.
Steve Sieting
(August 29, 2011)
Reference: Jeremiah 29:11

"Unconditional Gifts" is the cry of my heart when I felt like I needed to be more Christlike. The Holy Spirit was convicting me of my shortcomings and sin in this area. As Christ willingly gave all of Himself with no strings attached for me, I realized I needed to make a change. Jesus gave to me freely before I loved Him. He gave to me fully all that He had and held nothing back. He remembers my sins no more. Christ did all that He did to bring glory to His heavenly Father, and if I am to be a follower, I must do so likewise. I, too, must love freely, give fully, and forgive completely, because Jesus Christ has done so for me.

Unconditional Gifts

Search my heart for the gifts that I bring.
Let them be pure, not tethered by string.
Allow me to sow; let each field stand on its own.
Let the glory be yours and yours alone.
May my thoughts, words, and prayers be kind and humble.
Lifting up others and helping those who stumble.
The tithe that I bring, I pray you bless.
Obediently it's given, cheerfully acquiesced.
Work in me that I give not for a return.
But in childlike faith, it's your will I yearn.
Let not my gifts be reserved only for you.
But the very foundation of all that I do.
Out of love you always give.
So, I must follow by the way that I live.
It's not important that I be made known.
Only that you know me and welcome me home.
Steve Sieting
(October 9, 2011)
Reference: John 13:1-17

I used to be able to listen to Dr. Randy Carlson on Family Life radio at work, and he always talked about intentional living on his program. I wrote this poem based on what I received from his messages and what they meant to me. I came to this conclusion long before I ever heard Dr. Carlson on the radio, but I could not have laid it out in the meaningful way he does on his program.

Intentional Living

Intentional living, a disciplined life.
It's about changing habits, overcoming strife.
Choosing one thing at a time to change and grow.
It's no small thing, I want you to know.
Choose those things that honor Christ.
Overcoming is a calling to a new life.
Growth and knowledge should never end.
Look to Christ; He's more than a friend.
For in Christ all things are made new.
Live for Him in all that you do.
You'll never be perfect, yet peace you will find,
Because you choose wisely, one thing at a time.
Steve Sieting
(October 14, 2011)
Reference: Romans 12:1-21, Titus 1:7

A New Day

Darkness escapes and gives way to light.
The air is damp, the breeze so slight.
Calm water yields a rising mist.
Ripples emerge from tails of fish.
Streaming clouds dress the morning blue.
They radiate colors so vivid and true.
Nests awaken with birds hidden from sight.
Wings fan as they take to flight.
Leaves of trees turn to face the sun.
Dew drips off them; a new day has come.
Steve Sieting
(October 16, 2011)

The two poems about words are reminders to me about being careful with my tongue. Just because it may feel good to get something off my chest does not make it right, if it is done in the wrong spirit and at the wrong time.

Words

The spoken word is a dialect of the will.
It inflects its way and has power to kill.
Words are absorbed, repeated, and echoed in minds.
How long words last is not a matter of time.
Uttered in a whisper or stated as fact,
Once they are said, you can't take them back.
Holding one's tongue, not given to release,
Often is the best way for keeping the peace.
But words spoken in due season with love and respect,
Are words of life, and they have no regret.
So be quick to listen and slow to speak.
There is life-giving power for those who are meek.
Steve Sieting
(November 21, 2011)
Reference: Ephesians 4:29

Yesterday

Yesterday was seen by all, experienced by few.
We were so busy with things to do.
Focused on gathering what we have sown.
We miss life's pleasures and people we've known.
You went your way, and I went mine.
We manage our lives, but we can't manage time.
A second, a minute, an hour, a day;
One after another, they all fade away.
Time, we have, but we can't hold.
Slip away, slip away, the future unfolds.
Today will pile on the day before.
It will be yesterday, a day no more.
If you feel the same way that I do,
Let's pause to say, "I love you."
It means so much when we stop and share.
It's really the only way to show that we care.
Steve Sieting
(November 23, 2011)
Reference: Psalm 90:12, Ecclesiastes 3:1-8

"Oh, to Walk in the Woods" is about a time my spirit was crying out for rest. I did not realize until after I started writing this book that I was longing for the woods of my youth, where I often retreated by myself. I loved the wind blowing with the clouds passing me by in the sky. I loved to go to the pond and catch frogs. One day I thought I would kill frogs and have frog legs to eat. I went to the pond and killed several frogs. I skinned the legs and placed them in a bowl of saltwater under my brother's bed. My mom found them, and Gordon heard plenty about it. I could not tell you what I was thinking when I placed them under his bed, but we laugh about it sometimes. It may have been that "slow thing" I deal with.

Oh, to Walk in the Woods

Canvasing the ground, trees lumber a sound impressed by an illusory breeze. The corpus is touched, and clapping erupts as if leaves need to be seen and heard. They flap to and fro with nowhere to go and shred light's flight to cool the day. Light streams through, crashing to earth, and never a sound resounds. Speed is diffused, while the leisurely presence chatters away.

Never resting, always progressing, it eloquently ambles along. Carved by force, the brook stays the course. It pushes and pulls and gently flows, trickling where there is wake. Its lyric tranquil, a sound surreal, the heart longs to hear its voice. An angled look gives a reflective perspective that life offers differing points of view. Definition removed; colors defuse as they ripple upon the water. I stop and look at the person in the brook and can't help but wonder. Do I reflect or just project? What perspectives have I to offer?

Clouds in the sky drift on high, figures and shapes I see. Imagination at rest, I feel blessed at the wonder displayed for me. Skipping stones, I count each hop and always want to top the throw before. It is my work for the day, as it too drifts away, and I long to have one more. The calling rhymes as whispering pines compete with the song of each bird. Wings flutter on by, ruffling feathers as birds gather what they may. They remind me of me moving place to place, constantly having to fly. Nevertheless, I find rest.

Oh, to walk in the woods.
(December 25, 2011)
Reference: Matthew 11:28-30

The Atonement

Stripped of his clothes, they spat with distain.
This was the beginning, the crowd wanted pain.
So, they scourged Him as guilty, torturing His flesh.
They whipped Him thirty-nine times and not one less.
"A King has to have a crown," in a mocking call.
So, they crowned Him with thorns and punctured His skull.
The "symbol of shame," they placed a cross on His back.
Bloody and weakened, strength He lacked.
So, another person carried the cross up the hill.
This would be the last place His blood would spill.
Nails penetrating limbs secured Him to wood.
Breathing was hard; He did the best that He could.
He prayed for forgiveness, His work now finished.
With the crucifixion now over, the crowd diminished.
They pierced His side to ensure His death.
This they did to seal their quest.
The earth quaked; it had lost the Son.
The temple veil was torn; a new day had come.
Remembering what Christ said, "In three days I will rise."
So, they sealed the tomb, and placed soldiers at its side.
The Holy One had a plan all His own.
It was redemption of mankind, so He rolled back the stone.
There would be one sacrifice for sin, the atonement for all.
Christ, the perfect Lamb, had answered the call.
He is the risen Lord, seeking sinners today.
Open your hearts, and be forgiven His way.
Steve Sieting
(May 28, 2012)
Reference: Isaiah 53:1-12, 1 Peter 2:24

Words Beget Words

Words beget words: "he said," "she said."
They cultivate or choke by the way they were bred.
Release of peace that springs color to life,
Or poison that kills and brings nothing but strife.
This tongue of ours has power to sway.
It also has generational power that stays.
Being slow to speak is more than just wise.
It is far less sumptuous and saves precious lives.
Steve Sieting
(May 29, 2012)
Reference: Psalm 141:3

"Trails" is the realization that we all come from different surroundings and start at different times, so we end up following something or someone that has left precusory evidence in life. Yes, it may be confusing as to which trail to choose and what direction to head. But we have to make a choice, because it matters for our own eternal destiny and for those who follow in our footprints. There is so much political correctness that tries to invade our churches that it can hide the very meaning of a one true God. This poem was my way in saying I believe the bible as it is written. We should walk with God by the leading of the Holy Spirit.

Trails

Starting or ending is a perspective point of view.
Merging and intersecting, what's a person to do?
If I follow a path, am I following the lost?
Will I arrive at all, and what is the cost?
We pick a trail to see what's around the bend.
Sometimes we find our same footprints over again.
Trails are evident by marks in the sod.
There are no pathways that have not been trod.
We are all different and blaze life's trails on our own.
So many believe all roads must lead to a heavenly home.
I concur with this thought with a caveat that stands on its own.
It is Christ our Savior, the precious cornerstone.
You can know Him, do many good works, and say a prayer or two.
But if He does not know you, there is little you can do.
He will say, "I never knew you," and cast you out.
His Word is true, and He left no doubt.
More than just arrive, I want to get in.
So, I submit to Christ and find redemption for my sin.
I am a creature that has been born twice.
And it's all because, the sacrifice of Christ.
Steve Sieting
(June 5, 2012)
Reference: Joshua 24:15

Abraham Lincoln's Freedom

Imperfect freedom, by nature can't be one.
Imperfect in freedom, this country had begun.
Left unchecked for many a year,
That is until Abraham Lincoln did appear.
The country split into blue and gray.
Abraham Lincoln showed courage to lead the way.
He wanted freedom for all and a country united as one.
He had to correct a wrong that never should have been done.
The price was high and loss of life great.
And at the end, there was still much hate.
President Lincoln offered grace to heal the land.
This was not enough for a zealot band.
They conspired and took the president's life,
Hoping they could keep the country in strife.
But his ideals of "united freedom" proved correct all along.
They are a large part of what makes America strong.
Steve Sieting
(June 27, 2012)

The chair where I sit to read, pray, and write has a small shelf with a lamp on it and sits in a corner of my game room. After reading and praying, it is my custom to meditate for a while. It was during such a time of meditating about how much the Lord loves us that this poem, "Tapestry of Life," came to my mind.

Christ sacrificed Himself for us to save us from our sins. I know He did it because of His great love for His creation. He purchased us back from death so that we would have new life in Him. This is the very foundation of our Christian belief. Being a dreamer, the visual scene I received went beyond time on earth. I will be the first to admit I have no biblical Scripture to quote to make a claim that I know what the train of God that fills the temple is made from. What I am trying to express is that He showed me His love is forever and touched my heart with His fullness.

In Revelations 22:13, God makes a declaritive statement saying "I am the Alpha and Omega, the First and Last, the Beginning and the End," In 1 John 4:8, the bible says that "God is love" which means that His love is an everlasting love. The vision I received is that He wraps Himself in love. The very love of His children who sacrificed themselves in surrender and obedience to His will and lived for Him as Christ followers would be represented by a thread in His train that fills the temple. He will be able to point to the very thread that represents our lives and show us how He pushed and pulled us through life so we might come into His glory. I also saw very bright sparkles in His train and felt like they were also precious to Him. They represented the young and aborted children who died, not having a chance to be pushed or pulled into the fabric in His train.

It is my hope you can somehow get past all the stuff you have faced or are facing in this life and receive a complete perspective of the fullness of His love for you. No matter your sin, you can be forgiven. Place it at His feet, and leave it there to be seen no more.

Tapestry of Life

Time is a chasm between heaven and earth.
Its beginning and end elude the whole.

Threads of many colors, contrary to others,
interweave and a fabric is sown.

Close and personal, it looks like a mess.
Who can make sense of the life of mankind?

Events collide, disasters are sure to hit home,
for it rains on the just and the unjust alike.

Yet we blame God for all that befalls.

Can you believe in the tapestry of life and in a hand
that places and pulls your thread through strife?

It can be confusing as we weave from below,
but at our journey's end, we'll see time's fabric below.

Our thread will be shown as a part of God's plan.
It will be all about God's love and redemption of man.

The tapestry of life will be displayed in great splendor,
and each thread will reflect the glory of the Son.

His train shall fill the temple.
Steve Sieting
(July 3, 2012)
Reference: Isaiah 6:1

I don't claim to be better at this than anyone else, but I have watched people ostensibly disappear after a loved one dies and is placed in the ground. I became more aware of this after witnessing my father-in-law and mother die. My heart goes out to my mother-in-law and father. To me, loneliness is one of the hardest things we face, and they face it every day.

The Passing of My Heart

My heart has passed, the shell keeps time.
Life fills with wait, clocks still chime.
People comfort for a moment or two.
They're gone now. Oh, how I long for you.
Streets are busy. No one approaches the door.
Our house, turned into a home,
Is just a house once more.
Steve Sieting
(July 12, 2012)
Reference: Ecclesiastes 3:1-8

Compassion

Given to all and experienced by so few,
yet it's the very thing we were commissioned to do.
We are called to listen, to be moved, and love deep within.
Even if the pain suffered was caused by sin.
Looking towards others and lending a hand.
It should not matter if it changes our plans.
Stoop to help children, and comfort those who weep.
After all, we are nothing but sheep.
With ourselves on our minds, each of us has strayed.
Christ the Good Shepherd moved to show God's way.
It is not easy, yet it's the mind of Christ.
Tender in mercy, love willingly pays the price.
Compassion on His mind moved Himself to a tree.
The passion of His heart is to set the captive free.
So let us not follow wayward man,
but instead, simply follow His heavenly plan.
Steve Sieting
(July 27, 2012)
Reference: Colossians 3 1-17

I have seen excuses cripple as much as any disease, so I try not to make them. Honesty and not judging yourself, coupled with seeking the Lord's help, go a long way in overcoming. Once you show your determination is real, God will show up in a mighty way.

Overcoming

North, South, East, and West are for reference only,
and they're not a direction.
It doesn't matter where you came from, only where you're heading.
If attitude determines our altitude, who is there to blame?
Any excuse you give will only make you lame.
Life is about overcoming and having small victories every day.
Taking pleasure in the simple and those you meet along the way.
So, get up when you stumble. Keep trying when you fail.
If you don't overcome, you never will prevail.
Steve Sieting
(August 25, 2012)
Reference: James 1:12

Having experienced sin, I know what it's like to feel unworthy of God's love. I know what it's like to feel all alone, disconnected, and abandoned feeling like I was no longer loved by God. SIN is a real issue that we face as humans. Sin is so big, that is the very reason God sent His son to die on the cross to take our rightful place in death, that we might arise in Christ to a new birth by His redeeming grace.

In my opinion, sin and Amyotrophic Lateral Sclerosis (ALS) have many of the same characteristic's in how it affects our bodies. ALS causes the motor neurons in the brain and spinal cord to die causing muscle weakness. In fact, everything that the body performs on a volunteer basis eventually is affected by the disease. ALS causes breathing and speech problems and can cause Dementia.

Sin, is similar in these same things in that we lose the ability to speak up for what is right, our spiritual backbone is no longer strong enough for us to support what is right before the Lord and many times other believers. We lose the ability to relax for fear of judgement of the people that we use to talk with to the point we cannot breathe properly. The disconnect is a void. It doesn't hurt, and yet the void causes a disturbance within the mind which cannot express itself and so we generally isolate ourselves from others. There is a spiritual Dementia that occurs because we forget who we are in Christ. This disconnect left untreated through repentance, will close off all light from entering the mind until there is nothing but dark space, spiritual death.

Sin

Sin is the plan of a fallen angel who wants us to act without regard.
Two favorites at his side are jealousy and pride.
He is so cunning that he does not need to hide.
He pits one against the other for a web of deceit.
He'll do anything he can, so your soul he can defeat.
He'll even bless you with gifts that please your eyes.
They never last long; everything he has is based on a lie.
He has many tricks and snares to catch you in a trap.
He sets them all, because he does not lack.
You have free will, so you can't place the blame on him.
With the power of the Holy Spirit, you can overcome sin.
Steve Sieting
(August 25, 2012)
Reference: Romans 6:23

"Two Outstretched Arms" is a little bit of my navy life coming out in me. I love the word "fathom." I love that it is a unit of measure for depth and is based on the average wingspan of a man (six feet). I love that the method of measuring is through penetrating the unknown to seek knowledge and location. When I picture Christ hanging on a cross for me, I can hear Him say to me, "Fathom this."

Two Outstretched Arms

Two outstretched arms seem so little
Until you examine what's in the middle.

To a surprised, waiting love with open arms,
and to a fisherman who spins tales meaning no harm.

To a couple, it's a tender, loving touch,
and to a child, they show they love, "This much."

To God, it was sending His Son to die on the cross
and to ransom us, for we were lost.

Two outstretched arms measure depth and love.
Christ showed both, pointing to His father above.

To measure depth and love, fathoms are summed,
and when you look at Christ, you find He is the fathomless One.
Steve Sieting
(August 25, 2012)
Reference: 1 Corinthians 8:6

Taking a Sounding

When my submarine was on patrol and under water for long periods, the quartermaster of the watch would plot our course and speed on ocean charts of the area. These charts contain the lay of the ocean floor according to the latest information. Every once in a while, the quartermaster will petition the officer in charge of the control room to take a sounding to compare present depth to that shown on the ocean chart. Once granted permission, the watchman would transmit a narrow pulse beam toward the floor of the ocean and wait for the return, so the receiver could detect the echo. This information would translate to the ocean depth below the submarine and allow the quartermaster to compare it to the chart for reassurance of our location. If it was different than what he expected, we made sure to catch a satellite signal when we came up to periscope depth and then correct our position on the ocean chart.

It was during my prayer and meditation that my naval experience came to mind. We have to expend energy in the form of prayer to God to seek His will for our lives. Not just, "Now I lay me down to sleep" prayers. We need prayers that penetrate the deep things of our Lord, so we can find out where we are in His light and grace. Notice the energy was in the form of a pulse, which lasts a short time. The remaining time is waiting for a return to give guidance. This waiting time is much longer and done in silence and with little movement. Prayer is no different with transmitting and receiving times. They cannot occur at the same time, because a switch has to be changed to go from one operation the other.

In addition, since the pulse has a transmit time, there is a duration of that cycle when, if it hits an object at too close in range, you cannot see the object because there is not time for the echo to return to the surface. In other words, if you are not in deep water, taking a sounding by this method would not work. As I was thinking about this, I realized Jesus met me where I was spiritually. I was on the shore with my toes in the sand. Once saved, we are expected to grow and become fishers of mankind, and He calls us to come out into the spiritual depth and learn more of Him. Like many before and after me, I found I stayed on the beach too long, or I only went into the water up to my knees. And then I wondered why God did not answer or hear my prayers. Growing in grace and pleasing God are shown through obedience, and we will never be able to do so if we stay exactly where He found us.

I encourage you to take a sounding through penetrating prayers and then act on the return. The poem "Returns" is about this subject. I was led by the Holy Spirit to overcome my inward ways and lack of knowledge. He has called me to overcome spiritual depth problems by leading me on a journey to write this book. I do so in obedience to His direction.

You may find yourself in uncharted waters and find some underwater mountains. But it is far better to find the underwater mountains by taking a sounding than by running into the mountain without warning. Faith grows by hearing, and taking a sounding requires seeking.

Returns

Replies are result of energy spent.
Echoes return to the source from sent.
Soundings are taken to find the depth of the sea.
My prayers find the depth within me.
To get an honest reflection of faith in the mirror,
Christ you get when you invite Him nearby.
Revelation will show in love and not shame.
He only cares where you're headed, not whence you came.
Pray prayers to reveal your depth and direction.
The answer will be revealed with great love and affection.
Steve Sieting
(August 28, 2012)

Calling

Come unto me all who are weary and heavy laden.

Allow me to give you rest.

Love is the foundation of all that I do.

Life should be lived in the freedom and fullness of My Word.

In all that you do, do it unto Me.

Never give up seeking My ways.

Grace is given to you; do likewise unto others.

Steve Sieting
(August 29, 2012)

Very Few

Follow me as I follow Christ.
Who today doth proclaim?
We are all called to speak.
Who will say, "Examine me"?
Very few talk this way.
Who is confident to walk this way?
Very few proclaim Christ's name.
Very few. What a shame.
Steve Sieting
(August 29, 2012)

I talk a little about my depression near the poem "He Heard My Cry." The feeling that you can't be touched or heard is more than isolation, because others see you, but you feel like no one cares. I liken it to being surrounded by water in a bubble room that floats in the air, or a snow globe that only attracts interest when it is shaken.

Depression

Negative buoyancy, current lacks lift.
Avalanching inward, the shell exists.
Touch has no feeling; smiles have no face.
Sound is muffled, no matter the place.
Trust has vanished without a trace.
Who would listen about my void space?
Eyes in the mirror have a dim point of view.
They look back and say, "It sucks to be you."
Silence is deafening with a powerful grip.
Stillness is less exhausting, quietly I slip.
Existence is like a deep gravel pit and one stone.
In the midst of people, I'm all alone.
Steve Sieting
(August 31, 2012)

If you have gone camping and walked away from the fire into the dim light, you would have a very real since of what standing at the edge of light and darkness feels like. As a child, you can stand on the edge of the light, sense the increasing dampness of the night and wonder about what is in the darkness. Beyond the light brings a feeling of fear of the unknown, lying in wait.

Beyond the Light

The presence of light keeps darkness at bay.
Darkness is servile to light, and it cannot stray.
Darkness knows its limits and where it can camp.
The outer perimeter lacks warmth and often feels damp.
As light fades, darkness slithers closer to resemble light.
When light is out, darkness consumes all, and nothing is in sight.
Nature testifies, showing the contrasts we His people face.
Choose Christ's light, and live with His grace.
Steve Sieting
(September 9, 2012)
Reference: Psalm 1:2, Psalm 119:15

Prayerful Meditation

As I meditate on Your words and deeds,
Let them take hold; let them be seed.
Prepare my heart that I may receive
All the blessings You have for me.
Steve Sieting
(September 9, 2012)
Reference: Psalm 1:2, Psalm 119:15

I confess I have what I call a popcorn mind. There are times that before I can write down a thought, it is gone. I have always had this problem, and I'm sure it will not get better with age.

Fleeting Words

Fleeting words form a narrow beam.
They light the mind as they quickly stream.
Vanishing without a trace, they become far removed.
Escaping the pen, they'll never move.
Steve Sieting
(September 11, 2012)

I have a wicked heart by nature and fight many battles in my mind. In my past, I would have never said this for fear of judgment by church people and others. I've come to the conclusion I am loved by my Lord, and He is calling me out so others may seek the help they need to win the wars they battle in their own mind. You are not alone.

Formidable Foe

There is a formidable foe against me. We cast a shadow of one.
He knows my weakness and what I've become.
He knows where I've been and knows all my sin.
He constantly reminds me time and time again.
He has by nature a very wicked heart.
He has been this way from the very start.
I am confident I can overcome such a foe.
Even though he is knowledgeable as to where I will go.
The formidable foe and I cast a shadow of one,
Because it is I myself that I must overcome.
My flesh is weak, but Christ's spirit is strong.
In Christ I can conquer. To Christ I belong.
Steve Sieting
(September 18, 2012)
Reference: Matthew 26:41

Shortly after we started attending church here in Georgia, the Holy Spirit started working on me through a recurring dream, convicting me of my sin. Even though I felt led by God to go into the navy, I never committed my life to God fully. I wanted His blessing and yet wanted to remain the same. I would find out by His conviction that He wanted all of me. My dream made me feel very uncomfortable, and as my usual way, I would not talk about it to anyone. I would not come to an understanding of my dream until after my salvation.

My dream was that I was nude in public and everyone was unphased by my spiritual condition. I would be in the produce department of the grocery store, looking to buy food, and no one cared I was nude. That was until I saw the preacher come into the produce section. He represented the Holy Spirit and then my nudity mattered very much to me. I felt ashamed. I saw myself as being naked before him and tried to hide. He tried to approach me, and I fled in shame. After my salvation, the Lord revealed to me the Holy Spirit sees all of us completely for who we are. We cannot hide from Him. While the world welcomes you and justifies itself through comparisons, God justifies through His Holy Spirit.

The day of my salvation, I sat in the church pew under a very heavy conviction. I kept shrinking lower and lower in the pew. I finally gave in. I found it so hard to stand up and walk down the center aisle. My burden was so heavy that my steps were small, and I could not completely stand up straight. As I got down on my knees at the altar, I felt the weight of the world shed from my shoulders. I cried like a baby as He forgave me of my sins.

I Am a Believer

I am a believer. I stake my claim.
I place my trust on Jesus's name.
He talked with me and revealed my sin.
With nothing to hide, I was naked before Him.
As He taught me, He revealed Calvary.
And how sin had kept me in slavery.
When I saw the light, I knew I had been deceived.
All things became new once I believed.
Unshackled from sin and what was to come,
I'm eternally adopted into His kingdom.
Steve Sieting
(September 18, 2012)
Reference: 1 Peter 3:18

Only One Constant

The world spins on its axis, yet it's never in one place.
Tides rise and fall, while waves break upon the shores.
Water runs from mountains as it reduces them to sand.
Life springs, and life falls, returning to soil the land.
Winds spiral, scatter, and then return to a breeze.
This world is in flux, an ever-changing mass.
There is only one constant that was or ever will be.
I know Him as Lord, and He holds my destiny.
Steve Sieting
(September 18, 2012)

Vengeance

When treatment I receive is misplaced,
Grant me the strength to keep my place.
Grace and vengeance together cannot reside.
So, vengeance is Yours, and in Your grace I'll reside.
Steve Sieting
(September 24, 2012)
Reference : Romans 12:19

The parable of the talents brings this thought to my mind. While you can't earn grace, you can be thankful for what you do have by multiplying it for His glory. It is a sin to hoard or hide your talents. Where much has been given, much is required. God has chosen to work through His followers to show Himself to a fallen world. Talents used for His glory are important for His light to spread the gospel. It is picking up our cross and following our Lord.

Faith and Works

A candle without kindle only casts a shadow,
And a lamp without oil will not glow.
Barren fruit trees wither without purpose,
And a talent buried gathers no interest.
Motion without momentum always leads nowhere,
And momentum without focus is travel without care.
Faith on its own is a faith between two ears
And works alone glories for itself.
Faith and works are a conjunction with function,
And when put into practice, it is a heavenly design.
God will grow it; others will know it.
And many will glory in the source that is divine.
Steve Sieting
(September 30, 2012)
Reference: James 2:14-26, Matthew 7:21

Wicked Heart

We are wicked in heart with selfish lust.
We have so much want and so little trust.
Overcome this world I see as me.
Grant me, Oh Lord, Your peace and serenity.
Steve Sieting
(October 3, 2012)
Reference: Jeremiah 17:9

During a time of meditation after prayer, the Holy Spirit convicted me of my lack of faith for receiving from God. My past was interfering with prayers for myself, because I felt unworthy. He gently reminded me of how I had been healed of the disease sarcoidosis and that my heartbeat was back to normal. Faith is singular and not a respecter of persons. It simply is your trust and reliance on the great I Am.

Faith with Opposing Views

My faith has two faces with opposing views.
One is for others, that I believe as I pray,
All things I ask for will come their way.
I lift them up, and call out their name.
In faith I'm sure, and His Word is proclaimed.

My faith for self is a face of doubt.
Insignificant faith struggles to get words out.
My past rises while my thoughts roam.
I feel so unworthy to approach the throne.

Oh, ye of little faith, His words come to mind.
Know that I love you, and I count you as mine.
Let me help your unbelief and relieve you from stress.
I am the Lord, your God, come and enter into My rest.
Steve Sieting
(October 11, 2012)

This is my confession after dealing with a person who takes and never gives anything. It is very draining. After working with this person so long, I finally had this feeling. I don't claim it is the correct feeling to have. It is my honest confession of what I felt. It can be overwhelming at times to have such a person in your life.

Nothing

Nothing sown.

Nothing grows.

Nothing gleaned.

Nothing shows.

Nothing wanes.

Nothing remains.

Nothing missed.

Steve Sieting

(October 15, 2012)

My childhood bedroom had two windows. The window facing the east gave a view of our backyard and the farmer's field that bordered our yard. The apple tree and the sand pit just off the end of the house, where I often played as a child, show no signs they ever existed and have been replaced with grass. The north view was that of my woods, where I spent so much time in my youth. There is now only a slim line of trees, with a bike/walk trail on the far side that parallels the M6 highway. Everything else looks pretty much the same way it did when I joined the navy.

My Room

The room shows distress; the furniture stands alone.
Few ever enter the room that I once called my own.
Each time I visit, I sit upon my bed.
Everything is the same, down to the pillow for my head.
Youthful days started and ended right here.
The reflections are good, and I hold them as dear.
As I look out the window, I find the view is much the same.
I can still hear our voices where we played each game.
My things are gone, but I still search for more.
Just looking to look, satisfying the need to explore.
The feelings that surge are all tempered with age.
I moved out long ago, and life turned the page.
As I exit the room and close the door,
I know that when I return, I'll do it once more.
Steve Sieting
(October 22, 2012)

The poem "Conditional Man" examines my heart and the stages of my life I have been through. This is one of those private times in my life, when the Holy Spirit places a mirror in front of my mind and causes me to look at what I have been, as well as my current condition. I am imperfect, yet perfectly loved.

Conditional Man

Man offers conditional prayers looking for conditional signs.
Living conditional lives, we sit and opine.
We give conditional love and a conditional tithe.
We have conditional truths and tell conditional lies.
We want what we want and not just in time.
"Not your will, Lord, I'm comfortable with mine."
Man, judge's others to justify self.
It's easy to do when God's Word stays on a shelf.
Governments invade while the church sits in pews.
We think we're blessed, there's so little to do.
Knowledge has increased, yet man has not changed.
"Life for self" is the name of our game.
There is but one hope—God's Son, Jesus Christ.
Giving unconditional love, He sacrificed all and paid our price.
Steve Sieting
(October 29, 2012)

We need time to be still—apart—for the purpose of meeting with our Savior so that we can have a relationship. Other than giving my heart to the Lord, spending time in silence apart from my cares is one of the most important things I have ever done. Just giving time to be with Him so I could sense His presence and hear from Him. Wanting His presence in my life and knowing I need Him is an honor to Him that many miss out on because they are too busy. I have been in that same place, and the time I spent being too busy was for nothing. Now I have far more peace in my life, because He comforts my soul.

Set Apart

Pulling away to set apart,
The peace is tranquil.
When I think about my Savior,
He whispers when I am still.
Steve Sieting
(October 30, 2012)
Reference: Matthew 6:6

Having been in the navy, I've seen the beauty of the sea and the awesome power it has. She may look at peace, but that is very deceiving. With each one hundred-foot drop in depth, there is an additional forty-four pounds per square inch of pressure pushing inward. Seemingly at will, the waves can sink a ship, so you have to be respectful of her grace and power.

The Sea

Rip currents claim without permission
while displaying an ebb and flow.

Impellent constraint increases, and she obscures
while descending fathoms below.

Ascendancy atop acquires graves of deep,
and she may run silent, but she never sleeps.

Complex in nature and diverse in her ways,
grant her respect, for she's a lady always.
Steve Sieting
(November 1, 2012)

It is so easy to have a critical heart, because we have self-confidence that we could do so much better under the same circumstances. In my opinion, this area of judgment is the most overlooked, unless you are on the receiving end. Yet, I think it is the hardest to stop, because we are so comparative by nature.

Critical Heart

Honest and upfront, a positional claim
to state what they have perceived.
Stated as fact, the tongue is detached,
without regard to how it is received.
Their pride never sways as they impart their wisdom,
confident you'll come to your senses.
But truth be told, their words are cold,
and the only true revelation is that of their critical essence.
Steve Sieting
(December 10, 2012)
Reference: Romans 12:3

I have felt depression several times in my life. No one knows that you suffer, and you can't make a sound. Everyone seems so happy, and the pressure you face surrounds your very being.

My Depression

Isolated and alone the heart justifies.
The cry is softest at its fainting,
Longing for more, wanting escape.
Syllables form no words.
Silence's void is deafening.
Invitations are too heavy to bear.
Focused pressure surrounds.
The world passes by without a care.
Steve Sieting
(December 20, 2012)

I have worn every one of these titles and always come to the same conclusion. God still loved me.

Sheep

Self-centered, still I love thee.

Hard-hearted, still I love thee.

Exalting self, still I love thee.

Excluding me, still I love thee.

Promiscuous, still I love thee.

My love is perfect, everlasting, and fails not.
Steve Sieting
(December 20, 2012)

Man of Faith

Man of faith, yet lacking the same.
I trip over this thing man calls a brain.
Wants and desires sum more than my needs.
I take them to God and politely say, "Please."
He tells me to seek Him, and I shall find
More than desires; He shall be mine.
He is a God who loves and patiently serves.
He forgives my sin and gives more than I deserve.
His grace and mercies are new every day.
Christ is my hope, and His Word I trust and obey.
Steve Sieting
(December 27, 2012)

Nevertheless

You can have everything this world has to offer and still be wanting.

Nevertheless … God is *love*, and He gives you more than enough to share with everyone.

Satan can whisper in your ear that your religion does not work.
Nevertheless … you can trade your religion in for a relationship with Christ that will overfill your soul with *joy*.

When your world is full of turmoil and you can't find rest.
Nevertheless … the Good Shepard will lead you beside still waters and have you to lie down in green grass to bring your *peace*.

When a loved one rebels or trials seem endless, and you've given your all to no avail.
Nevertheless … God supplies strength for your *long suffering* with the hope of a good outcome.

This world will keep you very busy.
Nevertheless … you have the mind of Christ to lay yourself aside to *show gentleness* to others.

While others look after themselves and are willing to do anything for an end result.
Nevertheless … the character of *goodness* will be your witness in all times.

When intellect has valid points as to why your belief in Christ is in error.
Nevertheless … your *faith* and knowledge of what He has done for you give you confidence to stand on His Word.

When you are unfairly treated and revenge is the expected reaction.

Nevertheless ... you have the power to *humble* yourself, and let God deal with the problem.

Mankind is constantly being tempted to look to the left or the right. Nevertheless ... *temperance* will help keep you in fellowship with His Spirit.

Under the law, one can never meet its measure and remain in sin. Nevertheless ... God opens us from the inside, and we are beautiful to Him. His very finger writes the law within our hearts, and the "fruit of the spirit" is the evidence of His presence in our lives.
Steve Sieting
(February 9, 2013)

But Not

In the fire but not consumed.
Swallowed but not drowned.
Tried but not found guilty.
Yoked but not burdened.
Bewildered but not lost.
Surrounded but not captured.
Embattled but not defeated.
Perplexed but not confused.
Dead to self but not suppressed.
Surrendered but not enslaved.
Hopeless but not for Christ.
Steve Sieting
(March 30, 2013)
Reference: Romans 15:13

The Master's Hands

They are gentle and very strong.
They're accustomed to working all day long,
Calculating plans creation hews.
Elegant motion holds ambitions new.
Composed patience constantly measures,
Seeking to expose hidden treasures.
Unique is customary, orderly, and pure.
Outside unfolds, and love is secure.
In pain and agony, He lays Himself down.
It is finished; many gather around.
Steve Sieting
(March 30, 2013)
Reference: Isaiah 41:10, Isaiah 49:16,1 Peter 2:24

This poem was from a deeply hurting heart with the hope a loved one very dear to me would see all that has been lost, repent, and return to the family. I don't want my loved one just to be present. I look to the future with hope that they will rejoin the family with a loving spirit. I pray my loved one comes to the realization indicated in this poem and returns soon. I hurt! There are many of us in this same condition, longing for our loved ones to come home. Pray for my family as I pray for yours.

If you have left home after causing much damage and want to go back home, I hope you seek our heavenly Father. Ask Him to prepare your way back and to help your family be receptive to your return.

The Wayward One

I burnt many bridges and never counted the cost.
Surrounded by no one, now I am lost.
An island to self is not paradise at all.
I can cry out, and no one answers my call.
Having much, I wasted it in vain.
Much has left and is replaced with pain.
I must build a bridge to get to the other side.
I must build a bridge and swallow my pride.
I pray they see my determination and humbled way.
I pray for their grace; I need it today.
Steve Sieting
(April 2, 2013)
Reference: Luke 15:11-31

Waves

Waves swell and rise to meet the shore,
And abruptly crash as they roar.
Receding beneath, the current is hushed.
Nevertheless, it leaves in a rush.
Faithfully traversing, each wave chimes.
There is power to reduce rocks to sand over time.

May my prayers mimic the waves.
May each one begin with praise.

Swelling, rising, and praising entrance to the throne,
Let them fall in honor to the Corner Stone.
Under atoning blood, my sin is washed away.
He chooses to remember no more each time I pray.
Faithfully traversing, praying day after day,
He gives power to overcome, so my faith does not wave.
Steve Sieting
(May 9, 2013)
Reference: 1 Thessalonians 5:16-18

Life is absorbed through our senses and each event is given a memory location in our mind. Upon recalling of past negative events and feelings, we often feel unworthy to be called children of God. Our senses may have drawn us to something, but that does not mean we should partake. The mind filled with unhealthy memories affects our heart by making impressions upon it. These impressions burden our hearts to lessen our sense of worth in Christ. When we allow temptation to fester and develop into lust and desires, it becomes sin. This loads each of us down with burdens that we were never meant to carry. I encourage you to live a life of self-control, so that your heart is free to experience life in Christ to the fullest.

Since we all fall short and sin, Jesus provided a way out from the weight of guilt and shame. He simply forgives us. When I face the memories of my past failures and sin, I try to make the visit as short as possible so that it does not change my focus. I thank the devil for reminding me of all the sin for which I have been forgiven, and start praising the Lord for the victory in Him.

Impressions

Vision burns.
Sound echoes.
Smell allures.
Touch desires.
Taste thirsts.
Mind absorbs.
Heart's impressions.
Soul's home.
Makes sense.
Guard your Heart!
Steve Sieting
(June 28, 2013)
Reference: Proverbs 4:23-27

Resounding Voice

Resounding voice created a plan.
Explosive void made the universe expand.
One event birthed time and place.
And it reveals one origin in space.

Resounding voice says "I'll send my son".
Savior of humanity before life had begun.
Giving choice knowing we would fall.
He committed His best, giving His all.

Resounding voice of the Father, Spirit, and Son,
Humanity stumbles over three being one.
The Son shed His blood for remission of sin,
And the Holy Spirit came to comfort deep within.
Resounding voice works wonders before man,
Yet He simply refers to Himself as "I am".
They are two little words that say it all,
Meeting the needs of any who call.

Resounding voice's words of life endure.
They have no limit and, they are sure.
The Bible written by men inspired from above,
Yet tell a single story that God is love.

Resounding voice reveals God's plan.
God's simplicity confounds the wisest of man.
How one has the power to suspend objects in space,
Yet He whispers I am with you and works through amazing grace.
Steve Sieting
(June 30, 2013)
Reference: Exodus 3:14

My favorite words in the Bible are when God states "I AM". It's a statement of fact that says He is more than enough and that He is the beginning and end. He is more than enough, period.

Casting Shadows

Casting Shadows without the Son.
Advancing desires, sin was done.
Life without hearing answers no call.
Life without vision senses no fall.
A vessel at impact yields shards of clay.
Focus turns and searches for mercy's way.
Compassionately kneeling, the Son is made known.
He requests to make the broken heart His home.
New birth comes with forgiveness of sin.
Brokenness is healed and new life begins.
The shadow now cast is from His great light.
With eternity secured, the future is bright.
Steve Sieting
August 19, 2013
Reference: Ephesians 1:7–8, 1 John 1:9

Lord,

At times, I still placed my own desires above your will for my life. Please forgive me of this sin. I want to be led by your Holy Spirit and be grateful for your blessings. Thank you for your convicting power. It is pure and always given in love.

While reading a morning devotion, Haggai 1:1-11, the words of verse 5 captured my attention when the bible states *"Now therefore thus saith the Lord of hosts; Consider your ways."* The next morning, I awoke with words filling my mind. I pray each person stops to consider their ways too. I pray that God blesses this message to bring His light into many hearts.

Have You Considered Your Ways?

Have You Considered Your Ways?
Black and white is a well-defined way.
Interpretive opinions blur lines and inserts gray.
Lost boarders give room to roam.
In the shade of gray, many place a home.
Prayers without direction, receive no reply.
"God must be dead," the world cries.
Sacrifices cost nothing, convenience enslaves.
Tripping and falling, there is no light in their ways.
Dark, cold, and hungry the world is in pain.
Yet it denies the source where life is sustained.
God has a question that most refuse to hear.
"Have you considered your ways? I am here!"
September 7, 2013
Steve Sieting
Read John 8: 1-11

He Stoops for you

Darkness contrasts light.
Bottoms have the most height.
Burdens are loads without weight.
Tormented paths are not destiny's fate.

No matter the depth or how darkness abounds,
The Holy Spirit is present and wants to be found.
Look to Jesus, your redemption is nigh.
He'll stoop for you; He won't pass you bye.

Stones maybe in hand, but none will be cast.
When Jesus stands for you, they'll see their past.
Condemnation is a result of a sinful state.
Redemption thru Christ can be your fate.

Arise and sin no more.
Steve Sieting
October 26, 2013
Reference: John 8:3-11,

Hidden Stones

Cool and bright on a dry autumn day,
walking sod in a leisurely way.
Crackling erupts as leaves crumble by weight,
moving them closer to their inevitable fate.
Kicking leaves makes a rustling sound
and a visible trail appears where they once were found.
A pile of leaves tempts my eye.
I have to kick it. I can't pass it by.
Determined to fluff and scatter the lot.
The center of the pile marks my spot.
Swiftly kicking my foot did enter and
abruptly halts at the hidden stone center.
The day lost the leisurely and focused on strain,
every step taken was laden with pain.
When my foot heals, I'll walk in a leisurely way
and enjoy a cool, bright autumn day.
Hidden stones are on every life pass,
life is too short not to live it while it lasts.
Steve Sieting
November 11, 2013

Hidden Stones is an allegory poem about even the simplest choices that we make without thinking has a cause-and-effect outcome. Management makes choices that affect many workers, a husband and wife makes choices that affect each other and their children and so on. We have a sphere that we normally operate in and within that sphere, we have influence on others weather we accept it or not. Our influence impacts others in either a positive or negative way. Our impact on others may invoke an unintended negative response and/or judgement that could last a lifetime for them. Many times, we make mindless choices without considering the outcome or to see if anyone is watching, or if others will be affected by our choice. Many believe that's no one's business what they do instead of living like Colossians 3:23-24 ESV "Whatever you do, work heartily, as for the Lord and not for men, knowing that from the Lord you will receive the inheritance as your reward. You are serving the Lord Christ." This should be our testimony. In my youth, I was very shy and didn't ask questions, but I did watch and listen to others in the church and at home. I did so to learn what worked and how their actions and words affected others. I did my best not to judge them. It was my growing up catalog that I stored the information into of what would help shape my future decisions and thoughts. I didn't want to make the same mistakes or treat my future wife and children in the same manner.

Faith Must be Cultivated

Unsure of the step, still positive in direction,
Willing to walk with great love and affection.
Fields are prepared, stripped, and toiled.
Clearing the land and preparing the soil.
My time is now and this is my place.
Serving the Lord and spreading His grace.
He is Lord of all and a shepherd of one.
The harvest is ready, it must be done.
Yesterday's faith is in the past.
Yesterday's faith will not last.
Each field must be turned again and again.
It's essential for a new harvest to begin.
Daily refresh my faith and give me new wine.
Each day is new and now is my time.
So, I seek you every morning and follow all of your ways.
This is my love for "The Ancient of Days".
Steve Sieting
November 14
Reference:2 Corinthians 5:7, Romans 10:17

I felt led to write the following words as if God was giving me a message for everyone. I used the word "prosecute" in the second line because I believe that God knows that when we fully examine His words, they will be found to be true and pure and that our desire for the same purity in our lives will draw us into His presence. In so doing, we will find His wisdom and understanding. His voice will be clear and the understanding song will comfort our being. While God tore the vale at Christ death, we have a sin nature within our hearts that keeps us at a distance. We must make a decision to tear down the vale within our heart and become intimate with our Lord. His desire for us is as a lover and He longs for our desire in return.

From God:
To you:

I Desire You

Draw close to my ever presence.
Prosecute my word and incline thine ear.
Wisdom cries out to be heard.
And understanding sings truthful songs.
The heart has an intrinsic partition.
Its vale must be torn.
Enter in to my presence to know my voice.
My Spirit longs to be intimate with you.
God
Steve Sieting
April 22, 2014
Reference: 1 Corinthians 1:9, Jeremiah 29:11

This writing was inspired by the book "The Pursuit of God" by A.W. (Aiden Wilson) Tozer.

I found these words in Solomon 7: 10-12

10 I am my beloved's and his desire is towards me. 11 Come, my beloved, let us go forth into the fields: let us lodge in the villages. 12 Let us get up early to the vineyards; let us see if the vine flourish, whether the tender grape appears, and the pomegranates bud forth: there will I give thee my loves.

The Good Shepard desires to be with us and help us tend to the harvest loving us every step of the way.

It is my prayer that I keep this desire burning within my soul and like the grapes, my heart flourish in tenderness of new wine of the Holy Spirit. I hope you are encouraged to seek God with a close and intimate burning desire that can only be done in the spirit.

POEMS BY
ELEANOR SIETING

Despair

Despair, like a terrible storm wind,
Swirled 'round me and filled me with woe;
I dreaded to face each tomorrow,
So deep was the well of my sorrow.
Then hope, with a soul-healing blessing,
Came into my heart with her light
To bring me a dream of tomorrow,
To lessen my burden of sorrow.
At last joy has vanquished the tremors
Despair used to cause in my heart.
I no longer fear my tomorrow,
As hope now has banished my sorrow.
Eleanor Sieting

Grieving

The willow tree weeps silent tears.
The snowman stands forlorn.
They miss the boy of tender year,
Who played with them each morn.
His little wagon draped in snow,
The swing hangs limp today.
They watch, yet somehow seem to know
The lad has gone away.
Within the home, the table's set,
But still, it seems so bare.
Each eye is moist, they can't forget,
One lonely vacant chair.
I wonder, in the great beyond,
Where mortal eyes can't see,
If he will find loving bond
As once he found with me.
Eleanor Sieting

I Have Found a Friend

I have found a friend
Kind, gentle, and true.
I place my hand in His
To guide me through
To a better day.
I have found a friend
Who walks beside me
In grief and sorrow,
Helping me to see
The rainbow of tomorrow.
I have found a friend
Who helps me onto my feet
Even when I grumble,
Showing me tomorrow.
I have found a friend
Who knows me well
And loves me anyway!
Eleanor Sieting

Jesus

He came to the poorest of poor to show that He loved all men.
He spoke words wise, and He told them of their sin.
He uplifted the fallen unto new life and gave them peace within.
Eleanor Sieting

The Birth of Our Savior

The world lay in bondage and slavery and groaned from the weight of
sin.
The road of life was dark and dreary, no ray of light entered in.
Then one night in a stable, where cattle moved to make room,
Time cleaved in two by a wee babe, and the light of the world came in.
Eleanor Sieting

Love Is Like

Love is like a diamond,
Suspended between us,
Shimmering, sparkling.
Shedding its rays
Over our days.
Love is like a spring rain,
Replenishing the earth,
Filling our lives anew,
Giving rebirth.
Love is like sunshine,
Filling light's dark corners
With its sunny rays,
Brightening our days.
Love is like a rock
In a weary land,
Sheltering, shading
Solid, sturdy ground.
Eleanor Sieting

Noise

Horns blare.
Radios bounce.
Motors roar.
Fans hum.
Tempers flare.
Discordant noises fill the air.
Silence … There is none!
(Mom was kind not to mention her five children in this poem.)
Eleanor Sieting

POEMS BY
STEVEN M. SIETING
II

My Father

I am a man who breaks my back every single day.
I am a man who earns every dollar that I've ever been paid.
I am a man who lives the simple life.
I am a man who loves his beautiful wife.
I am a man who has been blessed with children.
I am a man who would ask for this privilege at any time again.
I am a man who knows that I have sinned.
I am a man who knows I'm forgiven.

I am a man who tries to live life right.
I am a man who fights the good fight.
I am a man who works hard trying to make my children see
That the Lord God Almighty lives in me.

You are the man I see in my heart,
Pushing me through when times get hard.
You are the man I want to become.
I'll love you always, your loving son.
(Father's Day 2005)
Steven M. Sieting II

My Mother

I am a woman who loves the Lord.
I am a woman who will sing His praises forevermore.
I am a woman who loves her children.
I am a woman who loves her husband.

I am a woman who loves living life.
I am a woman who tries to do right.
I am a woman who always works hard.
I am a woman with compassion in my heart.

I am a woman who loves to make people smile.
I am a woman who will go the extra mile.
I believe with all my heart that God is great.
And anything He asks of me; I will not hesitate.
Thank you for showing me how to enjoy life.
Thank you for showing me what I want in a wife.
Thank you for being such a great mother.
Thank you for loving me like no other.

Sincerely,
The Green-Eyed Monster
Steven M. Sieting II

MY FOOT PRINTS THOUGH LIFE

I concede adding a very condensed autobiography to a book of poetry is unique. In part, I felt it necessary to be more transparent and to provide additional perspective for the poetry. I also wanted to express that the journey of overcoming is a life-long inspirational walk of taking responsibility. Through exposing myself, I hope you look inward and then upward to your Heavenly Father.

Our Family Begins

Mom and Dad were married May 10, 1947, with very little to call their own. They were given permission to use an old shack out in the middle of the country for one week for their honeymoon. It was an old structure, with tin covering the windows and felt paper as the outside layer. It was in this shack, with no water or electricity, that a marriage of sixty-three years put down roots and established a foundation. My mom wrote a page-long letter about the fun they had during the week. They went fishing, and Mom had to clean the fish because Dad didn't know how. I like to refer to it as the "original love shack."

Mom and Dad had each other and a week together in this honeymoon shack to begin a lifetime of memories.

My mother and father were perfect for each other. They both came from families where my grandparents did not express love for each other or for the children. The family was a responsibility they tolerated. They were different from the way they were raised; they were fully committed to each other in every way. I count this as the biggest blessing and gift they ever gave me, because they sacrificed and made decisions based on that commitment, and it made my life so enjoyable. It was the living testimony of accountability to the family, lived in a simple and practical way that has made all the difference in my life.

My father was born to a family that did not want him. He was seen as just another mouth to feed. He does not talk much about his youth. My father is very reserved and never asks for much of anything. His father died of a heart attack when my dad was sixteen. Dad quit high school and later went into the army. It was after the army my mother and father were introduced to each other. My grandmother told my mother she would marry my father after Dad came to the house to tell her that he couldn't come over to see her that night. It was obvious to us kids that my father's mother did not like us as well. I don't remember a single smile. Her words to us were very few and never kind.

My mother's roots were troubled as well. Her father was a fireman and was killed when a fire truck backed over him when she was two years of age. Her stepfather was mean, crude, and did not care much for her or her brother. The entire family, with the exception of my mother, cussed, drank, and smoked all the time. They always scared me as a child. She told me that during the Depression, they often did not have much to eat. They either ate lard sandwiches or were put to bed to save energy. One time, a school official came to check on them, saw their lowly living conditions, and brought them some fruit to eat. My mother had to quit school in her junior year to help support the family, but before she quit, she made her mother promise to let her go back to school when things got better. She was out for one year. Then she went back to school and earned her diploma from Lee High School.

My parents' first child, a son, was born with physical complications and weighed twelve pounds. He died two days later, and I know this affected them deeply. They rented a house and had my three older brothers: Dale, Richard, and Gordon. They knew they needed a home with more room, so they started looking for an inexpensive home to buy. They found a small home on about a half-acre lot. An elderly lady financed the property for them for monthly payments of thirty-two dollars. My dad had to watch his pennies to make the payments.

The neighborhood was the real world to most everyone in the mid-1950s. Mom was pregnant with me in 1955 when they moved into the small house. It was located on a one-mile block that was shaped like a figure eight; my father lived there until his death in 2016. My mother was very short and large with my impending birth, and her sister, Peggy, was also pregnant with my cousin. They drove around the town together. Mom would steer, and Aunt Peggy would work the gas and brake pedals. Life was much simpler back then.

Father worked in a warehouse, while Mother stayed at home most of the time with my older brothers and me. She did work outside the home for a time when we grew older. We were very poor, and necessity was always the driving factor in the decision-making process. My mother almost died while giving birth to me. My delivery was two weeks late, and I was taken by cesarean, weighing eleven pounds, eleven ounces. She was told not to hold me, and because of her complications, she obeyed the doctor's orders. With a small house and four boys, Dad worked and helped the best he could. The next year my sister, Linda, joined the family, and she was the last of the children.

With four boys in one room that was not really a bedroom at all, my sister in one bedroom, and my dad and mom in the other, it was time to add onto the house. They borrowed money on the house from the same lady they made payments to when they purchased the home. The addition included an entry room with a closet and two bedrooms, one for my sister and the other for my parents. The four boys were divided two to a bedroom. My parents did a lot of the work with the help of friends. They had also heard about a garage that was going to be torn down; if they wanted it, they could have it. After dismantling it, they rebuilt the two-stall garage next to the house.

My mother told me that I was seldom held as a baby due to her health and busy household. She told me she could put me down, and I would stay in the same place for hours at a time and that I seldom cried as an infant. They fed me by laying me down and propping the bottle up with a blanket. We had a sandpit just off the back door of the house, where I would sit and play under the apple tree. As I got older, I was very shy and did not talk much to others outside the family. I did have friends at school, but not many. This sandpit under the tree, where I spent so much time playing, was my comfort zone, where I would often retreat to in my mind.

In kindergarten, I realized that many of the other children were much smarter than I. They could count, knew their colors, and some could even read. I was embarrassed and did my best to cover my ignorance by being quiet. I started living two different lives depending on the comfort that I felt to minimize being exposed. At home and playing games, I could be assertive, while in school and church, I would stay within myself.

Other things that contributed to my withdrawn state were just everyday events that got interpreted through unfiltered child's eyes. In second grade, I shared a desk with a girl. Class pictures didn't have names on them back then, but I think her name was Molly. I could tell her family was poor, too, because she always had to borrow my Crayola Crayons and other things. We did not talk much, but we got along well. During the year, she was run over by a hit-and-run driver. No one knew I was listening, but I heard people talk about how she was hit so hard her limbs separated from her body. The image of that in my mind bothered me very much, yet I never said a word. Her seat next to me remained empty the rest of the year. I have never forgotten her.

I seldom spoke in class during my elementary school years so I never drew much attention from the teachers. Several occurrences of an event during my third-grade year would make a lasting impression on my life. The boy who sat directly in front of me made sure of that. He was a tall boy, with blond hair and fair skin. I can't for the life of me remember what he ever did that was so terrible, but it seemed fairly common for the teacher to grab him by his jaw and shake him side to side, until he and his desk were both doing thirty-degree rolls from side to side. I became petrified. My eyes were wide open. I could see the hives break out over his skin. This happened several times, until the teacher became injured when she missed her chair and landed on her backside. She never returned to the classroom. I was relieved when I had heard she would not return.

Our house was the second house from the end of the block, with the woods just beyond the next yard. They would become my woods as I grew to play, pick berries, catch frogs and turtles at the pond, ride my bike, and find retreat for myself there. The woods were about one square mile, with about fifty acres of farmer's field just beyond the middle. During my explorations and berry picking, I came to know every inch of the woods. I picked berries for hours at a time, throwing them up and catching them in my mouth. One day, I kept throwing them higher and higher, until they were about twenty feet in the air. I about choked to death when one went straight down my throat. My eyes watered and all I could do was hold my throat.

Learning Life Isn't Always Fair

My dad worked at the A&P warehouse, loading and unloading trucks and boxcars. We attended the company picnic once a year at a local park, and they furnished everything. They also had first, second, and third-place prizes for the kids' games. There were not many kids in my age group, so they placed me in the next-higher age group to run a race. I saw the prizes lined up on the end of the semi-truck trailer. I saw a BB gun and a few other prizes and just knew the gun was for the first-place finisher. It did not bother me one bit to run against older kids, because I knew I had a chance to win. I knew I was fast for my age. The race was over shortly after it started, for the rest of the boys were not even close to me. I won and proudly waited to claim my prize.

As they announced me as the winner, the man handed me a stuffed rabbit. It was about one foot tall, with a plastic head and ears about five inches long. I was shocked. The BB gun went to the second-place finisher. I didn't say anything to the man, but this was one of the only times I complained to my parents about getting cheated. I hoped my dad would stand up for me and help me get the gun I thought should be my prize. Instead, I was told they would not have let me have the gun and for me to go play.

This rabbit stayed in my room until I went into the navy as a reminder life isn't always fair, and the races we run in don't always yield the prize we think we deserve. In my mind, the rabbit reminds me to be careful of what I give chase to.

Facing Myself as a Child

Quiet children do not ask many questions which hinders their learning. An example of this makes me laugh at myself now. I was sitting on the sofa, watching the children's TV show, Romper Room. The show's host would ride a stick-horse around. At the end of the show, she would look through a looking glass (it was really just a handheld mirror with the mirror removed) into television land to see all the boys and girls. She would say, "And I see Tommy and Sue and Billy," and so on. One day she called out my name, "Steve." I had always watched the Saturday morning TV in my underwear, and I was so embarrassed she had seen me in mine. Feeling exposed, I ran and got a blanket to cover myself. Then I took it a step further. I went up to the television—right up to the television screen—and looked at it from all angles to see how she had seen me. I never watched television again in my underwear until much later in life. I did say I was slow.

Another thing that makes me laugh now was my lack of understanding about music on the radio. My older brothers listened to rock music, so I heard different bands play their songs. Records never entered my mind. I envisioned the bands waiting their turn at the radio station to step up to the microphone and sing their song. Then they'd step back to let the next band have its turn. I envisioned that all the bands shared the same instruments. When I learned the truth, these things made me feel foolish, and I did not tell anyone what I had thought—until now.

I Learned the Value of Character from a Lie

In the sixth grade, I had to go to a different school for the first time and make new friends. It was at Townline School that I had my first male teacher. I was still employing my stealth tactic of hiding my head behind the head of the child in front of me to not be seen. I was in a classroom with a group of boys who were much more active than I was accustomed to. But as the year progressed, I came out of my shell more, mostly due to the competition on the playground during recess.

Having been taught respect and honesty from my parents, we were expected to act properly in school or pay for the transgression dearly when we got home. I was very good in the classroom, until I got caught up in some of the excitement the other boys were causing. The classroom had very high ceilings. And while the teacher was writing a lot of information on the chalkboard, several of the boys started to make the biggest spitballs I had ever seen. With their spitballs in hand, they decided to throw them onto the front wall, high above the teacher. The teacher kept writing, and we quietly laughed. I got excited and made a spitball of my own. The problem with my spitball was not in its construction but in its flight. I hung onto it a little too long, and it hit the chalkboard between the teacher's hand and his head. It made a splat about the size of a baseball.

The teacher turned around, his face red and his jaw muscles tight. He inquired who had thrown it, but no one confessed. He assumed the normal group of boys had to be guilty and took away their recess time for a while. They turned on me and said I was the one who hit the chalkboard. The teacher questioned me, and I denied it, which caused the boys to get even more upset. He believed me, and let it go at that. My fear was great, and I was not ready to confess my guilt. It was at that moment and the way my teacher treated me that I realized the value of honesty and character. I now understood what it meant in life and how you can stand on those values with confidence. This has helped me many times. I have tried to not take honesty and character for granted but cherish them as valuable gifts.

Making a Stand that Would Last a Lifetime

Picture four boys in buzz haircuts (I finally got to grow my hair longer in the sixth grade, which made me the last boy in class to do so) sitting in a church pew next to their dad, who has a little blond girl with a pixy haircut on his lap. This would be our family in church. We always sat on the right-hand side of the aisle, around the middle of the congregation. My mother was in the church choir and made eyes at anyone who moved. We served the church as a family by taking our turn at cleaning it every Saturday for a month.

It was during a cleaning time after I had entered the seventh grade that I heard a lady talk with my mother about how well behaved her family was. My mother received the compliment and happily added with pride that they did not make her children attend church.

I had a new best friend, who happened to be Catholic and attended Saturday mass. One weekend, he wanted me to come over and play baseball at his house on Sunday. I decided to rise up and declare on Sunday morning that I was going to my friend's house.

This declaration of freedom on Sunday morning was met head-on by a war of words. I was told I would be getting dressed and going to church. That aggressive nature in me took over, and I reminded my mother of her conversation while cleaning church. I yelled at them, calling my parents liars and hypocrites. I was mad, and there was no way I was going to church. They did not let me go to my friend's house, but I did not go to church, either. I stood my ground. I stayed in my bedroom, boiling over. As it got closer to time for them to come home, I calmed down. This was a good thing for me. My mother came into my room and apologized for trying to make me go to church after telling others differently. I accepted her apology and thanked her for doing so. It meant a lot to me. Her actions caused me to keep attending church. Even when I went into the navy, I found a church of our denomination to attend on Sundays. In California, I did not have a car for a while, and our church was twenty-five miles away. I purchased a bike and rode to the small church. I tried to get there early enough to cool down, wipe off, and change shirts. I also tried to sit away from most people, because anyone who knows me knows I sweat heavily. It was a hard Sunday when my bike tires went flat three times.

Junior High

Junior high brought new and exciting times in the form of team sports and I loved it. I could compete. I did not say I was great, but no one was ever going to try harder than I was. In the fall, I played intramural flag football. That winter I made the basketball team. I ran track in the spring and was voted the seventh-grade track team's MVP by the coach.

Basketball was the first time I represented a school on a team, and my coach was Mr. Batt. He challenged us to function as a team and learn a sport I knew little about. Being the second-tallest on the team, I played forward. I knew nothing about shooting the ball, but I was fast and possessed a three-inch vertical leap (this is my way of saying that I couldn't jump). Mr. Batt liked my effort and attitude and played me because of it.

We had a good season but lost to the same team twice by two points each time. We met again in the championship game. We went into double overtime and won by two points. It was the first basketball championship trophy in the entire school's history.

The best coaches try to instill life lessons and values into their players because they care for them and Mr. Batt was one such coach. After the game, Mr. Batt took me into his office and sat me down for a talk. He kindly told me how much more physically mature I was compared to the other guys, and referred to me as a man. He told me that I would stop growing, and others would catch up with me. It was obvious to me that he cared enough for me to help me prepare for my future. It was hard to accept, but it was true.

When we were done talking, I found all the other team members had gone to a local hamburger joint to celebrate. I lived on the opposite side of town so I did not normally have contact with my teammates outside of school. I was waiting in the gym for my parents to pick me up and was feeling happy but very left out. I had no money. It was the first time I remember hating being poor. The girl's gym teacher noticed, gave me some money, let me call my parents, and took me to the burger place. I was very grateful for her compassion for my feelings and need.

During a visit home while I was in the navy, I stopped by the junior high office to see if Mr. Batt was in. A student came into the office while the clerk asked for my name. When I told her, the student broke into the conversation, asking, "You're Steve Sieting?" I was very surprised someone would know who I was, especially since I'd been away from the school for at least six years. Mr. Batt was still using me as an example of my effort and the kind of person I was to him. It humbled me. I never forgot his talk with me, because it was true, and he took the time to prepare me for the future. It gave me a glimpse of two things as a young person. It was his observation, shared in kindness, which taught me about the power of observation and honesty. It proved to be useful in my future. I did not get to see Mr. Batt that day. I have never forgotten him—the way he treated me and what he poured into my life as he coached his team. I truly thank you, Mr. Batt, from the depth of my heart for your encouraging words and eyes. I hope we will meet again someday.

High School

I continued playing three sports a year and making just average grades. My youth leader at church worked a local grocery store's main office, and I asked him to help me get a job. He knew one of the store managers and took me to the store to meet him. I know that if he had not accompanied me, I never would have gotten the job. I mumbled and talked so softly my youth leader had to speak for me, because the manager could not hear what I was saying. In high school, I had one activity after the other and needed to work to keep me funded. It seemed like I was not home much, and I enjoyed myself.

As a sophomore, I had a very good year in football as a fullback and punter. I was voted player of the week twice. Going into my junior year, the coaches expected me to do well on the team. A spring training injury put me on crutches for a long time. My leg was hurt at first, but I could walk, so I did not complain. I saw the coaches talking with the team doctor, but the doctor never approached me to examine my leg or even say one word to me. When I went home, it got much worse, and I could not walk at all. My calf muscle felt hard as a rock, and the pain was strong. I used my own doctor, and I think the team doctor did not care for that. Later in the season, we were losing to our cross-town rivals, East Grand Rapids. I was still on crutches, and the team doctor yelled at me, saying that we would not be losing the game if I were in the game.

Being challenged like that on the sidelines in front of everyone on the team set me off. I told him I would play when my doctor said I could and that he was not a doctor. A few adjectives were thrown in for clarity. He was a doctor, but his field was in gynecology. He came over to me and grabbed me by the collar of my shirt. I grabbed him the same way. The stands were full of people, and I felt all eyes were on us. Someone separated us shortly thereafter, but the tension remained very high. I found it strange that not a single coach or school representative ever talked with me about the confrontation. The team had a different doctor the next game.

The football coaches never treated me the same way and my future playing time would be limited. At the start of football camp my senior year, I realized I shouldn't have gone out for the team. I played some and was the team punter. It probably did not help when the coach sent me in with a play, and his headset cord got caught on my foot. As I ran out onto the football field, the headset was ripped off his head, and he cussed me out. I have a nervous laugh, and it showed itself that night as I turned my head to see him. I was laughing pretty hard as I turned my head back around to run to the huddle with the play.

Lack of Reading Skills Catches Up with Me

English literature was a nine-week course. We had to read four books. There were no tests until the final, which would be essay questions covering each book. At the end of the nine weeks, I had just finished one book. I could not keep my eyes focused and often fell asleep or had to reread the same paragraph over to comprehend what I had covered. My mind drifted into another world, escaping on any thought. Today I refer to the way I think as having a popcorn mind. I never know when it will pop or what direction it will head off to. I met with the teacher in the teacher's lounge and told her I had only managed to read one book, and that it was the best I could do. She looked at me in the eyes for a short while and then told me she would only test me on that book. I was so thankful and walked away relieved for telling her the truth before the test.

I think I graduated near the bottom of my class. I joke now that I graduated 425 in a class of 413. At my high school graduation, all the other kids were happy and running around, screaming for joy, while I stood by my parents. My mom asked me if I was happy. I told her, "Not really." I told my parents I never wanted to graduate. They looked at me and asked why. I told them I knew I had it made in school and didn't want to face the responsibility waiting for me. I said, "Look at them. They have no idea of what lies ahead."

US Navy

After high school, I still worked part time at the grocery store, until I got on as a full-time position stocking shelves and working the cash register. I ended up working third shift, and it was then that my coworkers caused me to look at what I was going to do with the rest of my life. They said I would be there, just like they were, years from now. Though I had never been called by a military recruiter, like many other kids had, I felt led to check into the navy. It is what my friend next door and I used to talk about as young kids. He had a real navy hat, and we took turns wearing it.

I chose electronics as my field of interest just because I thought it would get me somewhere in life. I did not know anything about it. The navy recruiter told me I had attended a good school and should have no problem with the enlistment test. When I finished and they got my scores back, he told me I did not score as high as he thought I would. He started the paperwork, so I thought I must have barely made the grade to get into the electronics course. That was not the case. I went into the navy unaware of what I was going to face.

At Great Lakes Naval Station boot camp, my low-test scores were noticed during the several days of processing, after my head was shaved. They pulled me off to the side, while others kept processing through. I heard them say I should not be in the program. Since I had a contract and did not meet the requirements of the schooling, I thought that the navy would give me a choice to change schools or let me out of the navy. They never gave me that chance, and I think that was God working on my behalf. I think they figured I would not make it and have to be given a different opportunity in another rating for which my test scores were more suited.

After boot camp, I attended my yearlong basic electronic school, which was divided into subcategories like AC and DC theory. You had to pass each area with at least a score of 60 percent. My low reading skills and lack of focus presented themselves at every opportunity they could. I felt overwhelmed and struggled just to make a passing grade. It did not help that my first roommates were, as they put it, "cool." Two of them sold dope out of our room all hours of the night, and the third was an alcoholic. I was in way over my head and way out of my comfort zone. I wanted to return to my bed and the sandpit under the apple tree, but you can't go back. That never works either. I now realize while God was making a way for me to gain a skill, He used my roommates for my benefit I needed to learn to take a stand on my own for the first time in my life.

Struggling with school, roommates, and being away from home for the first time, I thought about going AWOL. But I just could not do it, because I knew it would bring shame to my parents. I went to talk to the school's leading petty officer, because he was next in my command. He did not want me to report the selling of drugs out of our room and encouraged me to say nothing. By this time, I felt alone, and the pressure was too much. I asked to see a psychiatrist, and they allowed me to do so. But by this time, I had lost my trust for anyone in leadership in the navy. I was afraid they would take it out on me, and I could not bring myself to tell him what I was facing. I walked out of the psychiatrist's office on the edge, and he never knew it.

On the edge and facing what was supposed to be the hardest part of school, I cleaned my uniform for the next day's inspection. That night, all night, another sailor knocked on our room window, wanting dope. I was so tired I overslept and missed inspection. I got extra duty for dereliction of duty. By this time, my sleeping habits had changed. I was sleeping stiff as a board, with my fist clenched, and I started grinding my teeth. I awoke just as tired as when I went to bed. This was the last straw for me. That next morning, while two of my roommates were still in bed, I got into the face of the other roommate and told him their drugstore was closed. There would be no more of it in my room.

While this fixed one of my problems, I still struggled with passing each area. I went to extra classes after hours for help, prayed, and held in there. Every class the instructor would take me aside and tell me I needed a ninety or above on the final test. Somehow, by God's will, I would just make the grade. On the last test in the last area of my basic electronic school, I finally started to perform better. These areas had performance tests where they induce problems in the equipment and you have to find them. To get an A, you have to find the problem in half the average time of the class, while the average test time would only yield a 90 percent. I was feeling good about how I was doing, when my instructor called out to me, "Sieting, what are you doing"? I replied that I was taking the test. He said, "No, what are you doing here? You're not supposed to be here! You did not have the grades to get into the program, and every instructor had written in your file, "He tries hard, but he's not going to make it." I knew it was only through God's help that I had made it through the yearlong electronic school. It caused me to recall how my seeking, led to prayers which led to the Holy Spirit encouraging me to step out in faith. It reassured me I was correct in feeling that the Holy Spirit had led me into the navy. I now count this as the major life changing event of my life, my moment in time that I realized that God moved a mountain for me. I had gone all the way through school hiding as much as possible, just doing enough to get by so I wouldn't be noticed by teachers. I had always lacked confidence in myself and God would not let me interfere with His plans to show up in my life and overcome what would have hindered me the rest of my life. He had to prove Himself to me that He would keep His promise and by doing so, He removed all my excuses not to believe in Him or myself. After the basic electronic classes, I went to the equipment schools for radar, receivers/transmitters, electronic surveillance measures, and submarine school, where I was always near the top of my class.

Mediterranean Operation

As I confessed earlier, my mouth can short-circuit, and things are out in the open before I even know it. At sea, one of my watch stations was as an electronic surveillance measures (ESM) operator. It involves listening to radars, watching a small screen, deciding if there is a threat, and reporting them to the officer in charge of the control room (Conn). Everything today is tuned quickly through automation detection. My boat was old, and I had to tune to the signals, find their pulse width, mix an audio signal with the radio frequency (RF), find the pulse repetition frequency (PRF), and time the scan with a stopwatch. Once I collected all the data, if I did not know the signal, I compared it to the signals in the radar signal publication to see if it was worth watching. I was pretty good at it in the areas I regularly traveled, because I memorized the sounds. But on my first operation to the Mediterranean, I was in an old and new world of electronic radiation, and I was unfamiliar with many of the radar signals.

Crossing the Atlantic was very quiet electronically, but when we came up to periscope depth when entering the Straits of Gibraltar, the electronic radar world was popping, buzzing, and humming. You name it, it was happening. Listening to all this noise in your ear for six hours at a time can get to you when the boat is counting on you for its protection. I did not remember an officer representing the Admiral of the Mediterranean had boarded our ship to welcome our arrival after we had surfaced. My ESM room door was open, and he walked in and asked me how it was going. I was in a panic and never looked up to see who he was. I told him if he knew what the heck I was doing to pull up a seat and help me out. He walked out, saying nothing. We were supposed to go into to port for a little rest before heading out on operations. That did not happen. Thanks to me and my mouth, we had to stay out at sea for an additional three weeks of training in the Mediterranean Sea. I was so glad the rest of the crew never found out about my error.

International waters are only twelve miles offshore and Muammar Gaddafi claimed the entire 350-mile bay as Libya's waters. So, President Reagan ordered operational training in the bay. We had several crypto technicians (CT) to aid in our part of the mission. Later, we saw Libya's submarine heading out of port toward the fleet in international waters. Our boat surfaced in front of the Libyan submarine and turned on our submarine ID beacon and then submerged again. Our boat returned to periscope depth to resume monitoring the environment. With a CT sitting beside me in my ESM room the a few days later, I saw a signal in a threat band that I had never seen before and I brought it to the CT's attention. The signal was emitting from a Russian-made MIG fighter jet coming from Libya. Our boat contacted the fleet about its upcoming liftoff. I learned later that the Air Force had a large plane flying in the area while the navy flew a F14 under each wing so that it looked like one aircraft. When the MIGs came close, the large air force plane broke away and flew back to base. One of the MIGs shot at our F14's and one of the F14 pilots shot them down. Before they could shoot the second plane, the Libyan pilot bailed out of the plane. In the submarine, we could hear the shots and the aircrafts hitting the water. (NOTE: I learned of how this event went down topside from the air force pilot himself. He was my CEO at the company that I worked for.) The electronic world I had listened to for days went silent for fear of our invasion. The only active radar that could be detected was that of the navy's F14s.

This action put everyone on a higher alert at their watch stations. Even with the increased effort, a few days later, I was on watch again when I heard sonar report to the Conn that a fish (torpedo) was in the water. It was an old-type torpedo and could be heard coming at us without sonar. I just sat there unable to move with my mouth open waiting for something to happen. It went passed us, and we got out of there before another shot could be fired in our direction. We never knew for sure who had shot at us, but I think it was Libya's submarine. This would be my last sea going tour of my enlistment. I decided to fly home to my wife, who was pregnant with our first child together.

Beauty pageant in the crews' mess onboard my submarine to see who would be King Neptune's queen as we crossed the equator.

I Met My Bride, Lynn, While I was in the Navy

Lynn was at one of our boat's basketball games on base with a friend of mine who was about to get out of the navy. At the end of the game, I took off my shirt to put on a dry one before heading back to my room. I saw Lynn looking at me and it reminded me of a cartoon character whose eyes bug out of its head, its jaw drops, and the tongue hangs out, while the heart leaps out of the chest. I couldn't help but notice the look on her face. I tease her about this every now and again, and we've been together ever since. I don't have the body I once had, but she still makes me feel good.

Living with Lynn can be entertaining. Several instances come to my mind that always brings a smile to my face. We were having difficult times, and the preacher had been preaching on casting the Devil out of your house with authority by telling him he had to get out in the name of Jesus. Lynn was doing just that while cleaning our bathtub. She was not loud, but I could hear her talking when I entered the bedroom when I got home from work. Trying to be caring and supportive, and not knowing what she was doing, I placed my hand on her shoulder. She about died on the spot, thinking the Devil was laying hands on her and she jumped out of her skin.

Lynn was used to giving Tyler, our oldest grandson, a bath and always fussed at him about how dirty his ears were, saying he could grow potatoes in them. One day she brought a potato into the bathroom and fussed at him the same way. While she was cleaning one of his ears, she let the potato drop into the bathwater. Tyler screamed several times while we laughed.

When we moved back to Warner Robins and started to attend church with Lynn's family, we lived in a small rental home on the north side of town. One day Lynn was in the storage room by the carport, trying to get something, and an empty gas can fell and hit her in the face, giving her a black eye. One of the men at church asked her what happened to her eye, and Lynn jokingly told him that I had hit her. He did not take it as a joke and offered to get several men together to talk to this Yankee about how to treat his wife. It took several attempts on Lynn's part to call him off, and I wondered for a time if we would still meet on the side without her knowing.

I used to get dressed for work in the dark so I wouldn't disturb Lynn's sleep. Sometimes my underwear was a little too holey for her liking, and she figured I should have already thrown them away. They were clean, so she would rip the bottom out all the way, fold them up, and place them in my dresser drawer. Putting them on in the dark was the easy part. But the feeling just wasn't what I was accustomed to. She knew when I had found the bottomless drawers by my reaction. She started laughing at me and said "That's what you get for not throwing them away."

Once you start grinding your teeth, you just don't stop when the pressure you once faced is gone. I overcame grinding my teeth with the help of my compassionate, loving wife, Lynn. One night I guess I was grinding my teeth next to her head. She just reached over, grabbed my jaw with her hand, and shook my head side to side, and said, "Stop grinding your teeth in my ears!" Startled by the sudden motion of my head being rolled side-to-side, I thought my third-grade teacher had gotten hold of me. I was scared and stopped grinding my teeth immediately. I may do a little on the side now and again, but never next to my wife. It's too traumatic!

At family gatherings, Lynn is the type who gets out with the kids and does things with them. Several times she has reentered the house banged up and bloody from crashing the scooter or something. One spring day I was taking the plastic cover off the swimming pool and cleaning it so it could be used next winter. We have a slope in our backyard, and the kids started sliding down the plastic as I sprayed it off. Well here comes Lynn in her bathing suit to join in with the kids. She gave it everything she had and was speeding down the slope—until she came to a sudden halt as she crashed into the side of the house. She looked like a mangled car after a bad crash. Every part of her body was bent. I sometimes like to refer to her as Princess Grace, with a smile of course.

Our Children

While the children were growing up, we were a very busy family, going to sporting events and active with church activities. We were firm with them and expected them to behave themselves. In church, most of the time all I had to do was point my finger at them to calm them down. For several years, all of us played baseball and softball at the same time, so it was a season of constantly running to and from ball fields. While we had a good time, I always regretted being so busy we did not take traveling vacations, like my parents did when I was a child. They were special family times, traveling to see the sites, camp a day or two, and hit the road for another park to visit. The family grew closer together because we enjoyed the time and we had to rely on each other. Now that my children are grown, it's hard to get everyone together for any length of time, and I often feel I let them down for not doing more of just family time. I hope when they read this, they will hear my voice and heart and make better choices for their families.

Mistakes aside, it is hard to form a blended family. I have tried to treat the oldest two children, Carey and Kevin, as my own, and for that reason, most people never knew they were my stepchildren. I have been with them since they were five and three years old, respectfully, and today they refer to me as their dad. No matter how tired I was when I got home from work, if one of them wanted something, I tried to meet their need. As a dad, there are many simple things that make it a good day to be a father. Teaching them to ride their bikes; catch, throw, and hit a ball; help them understand homework; and going camping. Things that help them grow are rewarding if you do them in the right spirit. To me, one of the best things is to look each of them in the eyes, smile, and let them come on in from the world and into your heart.

I used to hunt deer, and Carey always asked me if I had "caught" a deer when I drove up into the driveway after hunting. It tickled me that she would never ask, "Did you kill one?" One weekend I had caught a deer when my parents were in town. My dad and Kevin helped me hang it from a tree, skin it, and cut it up. While the rope was still hanging in the tree, with a loop at the end, I told Kevin not to mess with the rope.

When I came back outside, I saw Kevin hanging upside down by his leg. I turned around, got the camera, and took some pictures. Instead of getting mad, we shared some laughs. It was a good day to be a dad.

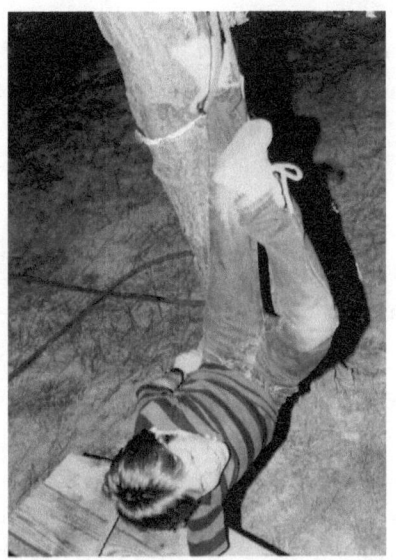

I'm grateful I took the opportunity to laugh instead of losing it over something small with my son Kevin.

My youngest son, Steve, was home from school and was bored and wanted to go fishing. It looked like rain, but I figured we hadn't done that much together for a while, and he does not ask for very much. We quickly rushed to load the boat and hook it up to the truck, and off we went down the road. On a long stretch of road only a mile away, the boat trailer tire went flat. The truck lug wrench did not fit the boat's lug nuts, so I disconnected the boat alongside of the road. Steve stayed with the boat, since it was loaded with our fishing equipment. It had started raining by this time, so I gave him an umbrella to keep him dry. On the way back from getting the proper tools, I could see him about a half mile away, sitting under the umbrella, in the johnboat on the trailer next to the road. I started to laugh so hard, because it looked so funny. What made it funnier was someone had pulled alongside him while I was away and asked him if he was having any luck. It was a good day to be a dad.

Looking back and seeing things as they were and are now, I can only offer a little advice. The first thing I would say to young parents is to love and guide your children. This can only come through prayer and wisdom, and you really get to know your child. Child is singular, because they are all very different. You can't mold them. God is the Creator, and molding an individual is accomplished through the work of the Holy Spirit. It's your job to give each child as many chances as possible to know His saving grace by training him or her in the way to follow and by setting the best example possible. You have to be committed to each other and let that commitment be made known as a living testimony.

Next, put much less emphasis on results and trophies and more emphasis on the effort and attitude while performing each task. Trophies sit on shelves; effort is a learned response in forming a good habit that will last a lifetime. Effort with a good attitude will help them transcend all other things they will face in the future. An old saying that for the most part I find true is, "Attitude determines your altitude." It is my belief this will also give your child the necessary mind-set to overcome failures that will eventually enter their lives. Many things affect our children, including the friends they choose, and you have to be their attitude meter and help them learn how to read themselves to make good decisions when they are out on their own.

The third thing I would say to young parents is help your children learn the power of a question. Jesus used questions to expose His attackers to their own prejudices. Always giving them the answer is less powerful than helping them answer their own questions. They hear the responses, and there is no escaping it. I also feel it gives you a chance to not react to a situation and allows you to hear from the Holy Spirit about what or what not to say. It removes some of the assumptions we make when we don't know the entire story. In today's world, it seems like everyone has an agenda, and they will get caught up in more than they care for if they don't exercise due diligence in seeking the truth.

The last thing I would say to young parents is to teach their children character, and words really do matter. If they are seen as a person of integrity, the child will be far ahead of most other children. Character has standards and becomes a foundation they can grow on.

Working after the Navy

After I got out of the navy, I applied for employment everywhere I could. Although my in-laws were good to us by letting us stay with them and I helped out at the gas station, we wanted to get out on our own. After a few months, I was hired as a maintenance technician, because of my submarine qualification card and all the systems I had to learn. The job was at the TRW facility in Douglas, Georgia. A few people talked with us, but most just stared at us, even when we looked their way. We visited a church for three weeks, and the same thing happened there. Lynn and I rented a house in the town. It was on a dirt road with a pond across the street. One day I came home from work and found Lynn in the corner of the bedroom, her back in the corner, crying pretty hard. When I asked her what was wrong, she lifted her head and said, "Get me outta here!" Luckily for us, a new electronics facility was opening up in Warner Robins, and I was hired. So, our stay in Douglas, Georgia, was just five months.

Youthful salvation is great and wonderful, with faith exceeding knowledge. That was exactly where I was at that time of my life. My new company was a good place to work, and I stayed for the next seven years. I enjoyed the many things we manufactured and repaired, and back then, we were paid well for the Middle Georgia area. I worked my way up to the lead technician. The Quality department started at a later time then the production workers and presented a relaxed attitude, coming in on schedule, but insisting on having their morning coffee and cigarettes before starting work. This made me feel like the quality department did not support our production since we had to have our station inspected before we could begin sell-off testing each day. I often interrupted this daily ritual in an attempt to meet production goals and my aggressiveness caused some stress. When you're young, you don't always fight your battles in the best light.

We got a new quality manager (QA), and he listened to other people, which did not help my cause. My supervisor started to have health problems and was out for a long time, so they filled the position with an engineer. I had asked for the supervisor position, but when you lack education, you will lose most of the time. He lasted for a while and then moved on to another company, and I finally got a chance to supervise. My old boss returned to work, so we shared the supervisory duties. I attended the manager's status meeting for production, because I knew every item in the shop without a single note in front of me. We were under pressure to get production out, and the facility manager was pushing for answers. The QA manager made a remark about it was all production's fault. My mouth started in motion, with no filter installed. I told him we could not get QA support, because they spent so much time in the break room that I thought they were statues, and I had walked around them all this time. With this comment, the war was on, and anger was high. I got support, just not good support. It was not long after that my manager left the company, and you can only guess who got his job. Yes, the QA manager.

With the QA manager as my new boss, I was relieved of my supervisory duties and put back to technician's work and programming the new cable-bending machine. I kept to myself and just worked. It did not take long for my manager to be pressured by the facility manager for answers to which he received none. Production was very low, so my manager called me to his office and closed the door. I thought I was going to be passing through it on my way to the HR department, with a pink slip in hand. But that's not what happened. He told me he had been looking for answers from the other two supervisors and had bought into all the lies talked about me. He told me, "We're going to have a meeting, and everything that is going to be said does not pertain to you." He apologized and gave me credit for keeping my work flowing. I simply told him that when I came here to work, I gave my word to do the best job I could, and it did not depend on who I worked for. It was simply my word. He told me I was a better man than he was. From that point on, he and I worked very well together, and I ran the lab operations from that day forward.

One Bad Apple

We had one lady who was treated very well by my previous boss, to the point she thought she could work at her leisurely pace, come in late, and then stand around and talk. I learned she had sued the company about a neurological disorder due to the Freon used in the plant messing up her brain. The trouble was she already had a documented neurological disorder before she came to work. She lost that case but was winning at the end of every divorce. Her father died in a truck crash, and she attempted to have her mother committed to get the approximately $250,000 in settlement money. This lady never broke stride of finding a way to get something for nothing. Little did I know I would the focus of her next attempt at financial gain.

As her supervisor, I knew the type of person she was and had a fear of even talking to her. But I had to treat her the same way as everyone else and direct her work. Her time cards started having errors on them every week. Finance had to have them corrected before I went home so they could complete their work. I had to figure out what units she worked on by the folders in her area and the signatures on them and then correct and initial the time cards. The old-time cards were kept in a filing cabinet in the hallway, and no one knew that she was going to the file and making copies of her changed time cards. On top of this, she was asking every question under the sun of what to do, how to do it, and what to charge her time to. The questions were common knowledge to anyone who had worked there for just a couple of weeks, and this was her seventh year. With every question she asked, I felt the Holy Spirit guide me to reply with a question of my own. She had to give an answer, and this saved me later.

Having had my fill of all the stuff and time cards problems, I called her to my office told her she needed to put her head back on her shoulders and perform to her rate of pay. If not, I would take further actions to discipline her. She looked right at me and said slowly, with hatred in her eyes, "You don't intimidate me," and walked out. Two days later, the company, my manager, and I were being sued for stressing her out. Her lawyer and gynecologist, joined together to form her legal team. It was at this point I realized my track record with gynecologists was not too good.

The Secret Informant

Some employees told me she was going to dance on my grave and wouldn't have to work for the rest of her life. Her plans started to be unveiled before my manager, and he shared them with me. A friend she thought she could trust had called my manager, letting her know what was going on. This was when we found out she had copied the time card corrections I made. She had called the Military Investigation Service as a whistle blower and turned me in for time card fraud by charging to different contracts. If proven in court, I could have been sentenced to serve jail time. Can I tell you, even when you know you're innocent, it is very terrifying and stressful wondering how you can prove what really transpired. Day after day, one thing after another would unfold. We even knew when she would meet the Military Investigation Service in the Kroger parking lot on Russell Parkway to turn over her records. The Military Investigation Service came to our facility but never talked with me. It cleared the company and me of any wrongdoing, but we did have to change our time card procedures.

Cleared of one issue, I still faced a lawsuit over the stress of my employee. The secret informant told us how the lawyer and doctor were bolstering their case. My former employee was showing this person everything she had in her files and bragging about it. The informant must have played along very well and for a reason I have never found out. Before the lawyers brought the case to a judge so they could start taking depositions, the informant stole the package of documents out of my former employee's house. She called my manager and told him to pick up a package at Hardees. She told him to ask for a package at the counter. My manager sent me to pick it up. I didn't know what I was picking up, only that it was from the informant. All the documents supporting her case were in that package. The next day, the informant called to let us know the employee was furious, and the police had been called. She warned us that I was considered the prime suspect for breaking in and taking the documents.

As if all the stress wasn't enough for one person, it was during this time that I had also been exposed to a chemical that made it so I could not breathe for some time. At the time of the chemical exposure, all I could do was stand there and suffocate. It felt like a very strong man had wrapped his arms around me so hard that I could not expand my chest to take a breath. I took a lung test for work prior this exposure. Several pulmonary tests that I took after this event showed that I had lost 64 percent of lung capacity.

Enough Was Enough

A management person had not charged his time properly, logging a lot of time to fixing the test stations we used every day. When our contract was up for bid, which had been a sole-source contract with the government, the company used actual figures to bid for the contract. The government saw the quote of about ten thousand dollars a month to maintain the station, and they opened it up to small businesses. We lost the main source of our work. With no large contract, coupled with several lawsuits, the company began plans to close our facility and move our jobs to California. I helped several of my employees get a job with a contractor on the other side of town. I helped train people in California to do our old jobs until I was laid off. I ended up working for the same local contractor where I had aided several of my former employees get a job. It would only take me a couple of days to realize I did not like the place, but I needed the work and stayed there four and a half years—in misery. Shortly after I started work on my new job, I had to take time off twice to testify at a disposition and find a lawyer.

The first deposition was just me, the company lawyer, her attorney, and his recorder. I kept my answers as short as possible, and if it was a poor question, I made them clarify the question so it would be specific. I did not want to answer a question one way and find out they meant something else. The company attorney liked the way that I had handled myself and convinced the company to pay my attorney fees.

The second deposition was with my ex-employee present. My mother always told me not to start a fight, but if I got into one, I'd better finish it. This was my mindset on this day. I wanted to verbally kick their tails, and I took my shots every chance I could. The judge who was going to read this statement would not have to read between the lines, because I was going to spell it out for them. They were looking for the secret informant and anything else that would strengthen their case. Since I had heard her voice a time or two and picked up the package at Hardee's, they probed hard into these areas.

Her lawyer made the mistake of asking for my opinion, and I expounded much further than they cared for. I can honestly say I get this from my mother. I wanted to make sure the judge knew exactly what kind of person she was. I told of her other lawsuits, which included trying to have her own mother committed so she could claim the insurance settlement money, and the false Freon case, when she already had a neurological disorder. I told them these things were not hearsay, because they were her very own words. I ended my speech with, "In my opinion, she is a person of very low character and will do anything she can to get money for nothing." I told them I had written down our last conversation, and it had ended with, "You don't intimidate me." This was their entire case, and it was now gone. The judge dismissed the case not long afterward. The poem "Go before Me, Lord, This I Pray" is how I felt and what I prayed during this time of my life. I looked at Scriptures for God fighting my fights, and I wanted His intervention.

A Decision Does Not Always Mean It's Over

After being so bold during the depositions and being delivered from the Military Investigation Service and the lawsuit, you would think I would be on top of the world. That was not the case. My new job was for half the pay, I started having vertigo often, and my children started going wild. With so much stress and turmoil, I had stopped praying and reading my Bible. There just did not seem to be time for it, and yet it was the thing I needed most. It would not be long before I started to have kidney stones, and during a chest X-rays, a mass was discovered. I had a lung and a lymph node biopsy, and with a lot of blood work, the doctors determined I had sarcoidosis. I was told is not the same for everyone. In my case, the sarcoidosis covered my heart, and my heartbeat was so strong it felt as if it was going to leap out of my chest. I became very tired and ran out of breath quickly. For a while, I thought I was going to die. I was referred to a heart specialist and monitored. He attempted a heart ablation, and when that failed, I went on medication to control my heartbeat.

I felt we were doomed to this type of life for the rest of our lives. With our children, we went through attempted suicide twice and several arrests. One child was finally diagnosed with bipolar disorder. The extreme highs and lows experienced by the individual and by those on the receiving end made it feel as if there is no such thing as a normal day. At times, I felt I was being sifted as wheat, with the Devil standing by, watching and laughing. People would come up to us and tell us we had inspired them for enduring so much while smiling. I wanted to tell them that was never our intention, but we simply replied with a thank-you. And to top off our problems, the church we attended for about fifteen years fell apart due to staff infighting and betrayal. We started going to another church, but when you're low in spirit, you can't always hear the messenger. All this went on for at least ten years, and I was now empty of living water in my soul.

It would be easy to claim all the trials and problems we faced that ushered me into depression were understandable after enduring so much for so long. But that would be another excuse. I failed in my relationship with the Lord. It's just that simple. God did not change. I had allowed the pressures of life push me away from Him. At the very moment I had made up my mind to quit faking my religion and give up because I had had enough, I let out one last short prayer, and then went silent. At that very moment, God said to me, "I hear your cry." He knew I was serious about walking away without turning back, so He reached out for me and assured me He is real and did care for me. I speak about this more in detail near the poem "He Heard My Cry" and the drowning I was about to have spiritually. God pulled me up from certain death with four little words. Today, I stand with confidence on those four words that I am not alone. I have a personal Savior who truly loves me. God loves you just as much. Don't let life push you into becoming a spiritual drowning fatality.

A Few Additional Thoughts

Over the years, I found that God made me recall events as pictures in my mind that bring His nature to light or expose myself as I am so that He can do a work in me in a gentle, loving manner. I count it as a gift of love. He relates to my present-day struggles with a past experience or something from the Bible I can relate to. He lays it out in my mind in a way that it brings me pleasure, understanding, and clarity to complete a good work in me. I would like to share some of these moments with you. Some of them were before I had sinned and felt God was not real anymore. I sometimes wonder how I could have been so shallow to turn and walk away from Him.

Bumps and Potholes in the Road of Life

As a young Christian, I found myself struggling to overcome all my sinful ways and bad habits all at once so I could fit into the church the way I thought I should be. These bad habits and sins that I had acquired over my life did not just fall away at my new conversion. I would sometimes become frustrated with myself for committing the same errors over and over again. The Holy Spirit brought to my mind the image of a bike I had growing up. It was an old English Racer, and I felt very fast on that bike. It had one problem that I did not understand the cause of or know how to correct it at the time. But I became keenly aware of the results of the problem. The spokes on the front wheel rim were loose, and every time I hit a pothole or a large bump, the front wheel collapsed, and I went flying over the handlebars. Now this was before helmets, so I took some nasty falls. I also told you I was a little slow in the head, so this never stopped me from using the bike. I would get up, place the bike wheel between my thighs, and squeeze my legs together until the wheel popped back into shape. Then I continued on my way.

As I pondered why God brought the bike to my memory, He gently reminded me of the potholes in the road. I would have to face roads I was never on before and would not always know the road conditions. Trying to avoid them was not the real solution. Getting a new bike rim or tightening the spokes to make the wheel aligned and true would be the real solution to my problems. He let me know He would work with me to correct my ways one at a time so that I could overcome my bad habits through Him. He then took my mind to a farmer's field that looked like it was almost ready to harvest. The wheat looked even and consistent throughout the field. Some weeds stood proudly in the middle of the field. He let me know that if I were to go out into the field before it was time to harvest just to remove the weeds, I would cause much more damage to the crops than if I waited until after the harvest. After the harvest, no crops would be lost, and the weeds would be exposed and easily removed. If I could be patient with Him, He would be Lord of my harvest and help me with all my bad habits when the time was right.

While He is Lord of our personal harvest, we must remember this is also true for everyone else. They can see the weeds in their own fields; they don't need you to point them out. We are called to love and witness, and let God's Word and Holy Spirit do the inner working of humankind.

Cans Alongside the Road

In the mid-1990s not many people collected aluminum cans, and our Royal Ranger group collected them to support our group activities. During this time, you saw all kinds of trash along the roadside in Georgia. When I was driving home from work, I noticed quite a few cans on the roadside near my house. I got up early one Sunday morning and went for a jog before church. I took along some large trash bags, and in just one mile, I had completely filled one bag. I thought, I'd better turn around and pick up the other side of the road. With two bags full of aluminum cans, I was pleased with my efforts to support our program. My self-satisfaction soon left me, when I felt the Holy Spirit say the cans were only a small representation of lost souls I passed by every day.

The revelation from the Holy Spirit was meant to open my eyes to the world around me. It did, but it should not have stopped there. I wish I could say I went on the move for Christ and sought His direction in reaching the souls I passed in my daily travels. But I kept my place and will have to give an account for my sins of omission. I am making an effort to conform to His image so that this will not be an event repeated throughout my lifetime.

This part of my life and the event made me think of when we come face-to-face with our Lord. The Bible gives a sense of how terrible it will be, because He is the great I Am. Our righteousness will be filthy in comparison to Him. We will be afraid to enter, yet enter into His presence we must. The Bible also talks about the Lamb's Book of Life, and if our name is written in it, we will enter into the joy of the Lord. This made this day dreamer dream about this upcoming event. Since we are made in God's image, our souls will no doubt return to Him. The skin is human's largest organ. What if the skin of our soul was the largest part of our soul as well and God's Book of Life for our personal life? I pictured every sin and idle word tattooed in red onto the skin of our soul. With salvation and repentance, everything that was sin is washed away by the blood of Christ, and only the good we did and the sin that was not placed under the blood would be read like a book from our tattooed souls. There would be no argument, because we are our own tattoo artists. It would be a terrible event to face the Lord covered not by the blood but by tattoos recording our sins.

I know this picture has no biblical basis, yet is has brought to light—in terms I can better understand—the need to repent of my sins and obey the Lord, my God. I cannot take this lightly. I hope this makes you face yourself in the spiritual mirror and take a good look at your soul. Make sure it is completely washed by the blood of the Lamb. The Holy Spirit should be welcome in every chamber of your heart and have the freedom to live and move and have its being as Lord of all. Yes, it will be terrible to come face-to-face with our Lord, but it does not have to be tragic as well.

Certification

I have been a certified solder trainer for years now. In order to do so, you have to agree to follow all processes, procedures, and training material. There can't be any substitute or variation. Recertification is required every two years. You have to respect the process because not everything can be viewed by inspection. During my studies of the requirements, I often thought that Christian's ought to have a certification program. I've often thought that it's not enough to be saved. There has to be more to the Christian life.

Like the solder connection, not everything in our lives can be inspected. We don't treat everyone in the same way and we wear a façade on our faces. After many times of recertifying as a solder instructor, I felt like God did have a certification program, and it's called discipleship.

In order to be a disciple, you have to fully submit to the Lord and follow His policies and procedures as stated in the bible. There can be no substitute. I sometimes think that the church as a whole, stops at salvation and doesn't encourage growth to reach discipleship. Reference: John 8:31 and Luke 9:23

Solder Connections

I'll give an example of what happens when a solder joint is not made properly. When a wire is clinched to the post after it has been pretinned with solder. The wire is then wrapped securely around the post so that it won't move. A solder bridge is formed by placing solder between the wire and the soldering iron. To make a good solder connection , the wire and post must remain still during and after the soldering procedure until the solder has solidified.. The solder connection should be shiny and smooth. A good connection will allow electricity to flow smoothly through the solder joint with no voltage drop.

If the wire and or post move during the process, especially during solder solidification, the solder joint becomes a disturbed solder connection, (in earlier times, these were called a cold solder joints). It might pass electrical tests for a while and fail later. Electricity will not flow smoothy through a disturbed solder connection. The electrons will move side to side fighting their way through the connection. This action causes a voltage drop (heat in the connection) that shouldn't be there and it changes the circuit's characteristics. These failures are hard to detect and therefore become costly to the manufacturer.

How many people are moving when God is using a refining fire on us? Instead of trusting God for our good, we quickly become impatient and start complaining while we fidget hoping to find our own comfort. There are a lot of people with disturbed connections to God that wonder why their prayers go unanswered or even where God is in their lives.

Another type of connection is a screw and terminal post connection. One of the places I worked at had large power supplies that drove the production line. One day it stopped all of a sudden. I could hear a noise coming from within the cabinet. I opened the cabinet door and witnessed electric blue fire balls shooting all over the place. The screw connections weren't properly torqued. Once they heated up to a certain point, arcing started. We shut the line down and tightened every connection and restarted the unit.

These two examples are just a sample of connections in electronics and is also representative of so many people living today. We pray for blessings and yet we won't even try to make a good connection to touch the Lord with our hearts, obedience, and love for others that we can make a difference in their lives. Like the disturbed solder connection, our connection was made without following God's process to draw near to Him. Our connections don't allow for Him to freely communicate with us because we failed to obey and follow the process. I'm glad that we no longer live in the Old Testament days when I think about Uzzah trying to steady the Ark when it was about to fall as told in 2 Samuel 6:3-8, and it killed him because Uzzah violated the divine law.

Dachshund Leason

I believe that our connection to Christ has to be the most important thing that we seek (reference Matt. 6-33). The bible does have a process to follow to draw closer to God. I'll give one more story that made me think about my connection to the Lord.

We had a dachshund dog that we named Lewis. He loved to be touched and to touch us. Once, in the backyard, when he saw me and I called for him to come to me. He ran with happiness on his face that was evident to me. He came most of the way and stopped and laid down on his back for me to go to him and rub his belly. I called several times trying to get him to come the rest of the way, but he never did. He got distracted by something else and he went off to find it.

It made me wonder how many times that I did something similar when the Lord called for me to come to Him. I get distracted and don't go far enough and just like my dog, Lewis, I leave before God can bless me. I think that there is a difference in coming "to" the Master and coming "unto" the Master. The dictionary defines the word unto as "until + to". I look at it like my dog, he came "to" me yet not close enough for me to touch. When you go unto the Lord, you get close enough to touch Him and for Him to return your love.

Power of your prayer

The thing about prayer is that there are many different types of prayers. God has many names and each name of God has its own character, meaning and power. And like the names of God, our prayers have similar traits because we were created in His image. But there is one trait of the names of God that we often overlook and that is, *God is personal.* The most important thing to God is that you are submissive and supportive of His love which involves getting to know him on a personal level. I know many will read this and will say that they pray, read the bible, and walk by faith, so this word is not for me. May I ask you one question? When have you last heard the voice of God speaking to you? This is personal because it has everything to do with your relationship with your Lord. In John 10:27, Jesus says "My sheep listen to My voice; I know them, and they follow me." Hearing the Lord speak to my soul is my assurance that I have a relationship with Him.

So how does one create an effective powerful prayer life that has a personal impact? Psalm 130:5, says it like this, *"I wait for the LORD, my soul doth wait, and in his word do I hope"*. Notice that the inner most being waits for the Lord and that they have placed their trust in His word. When you have taken the time to place the word of God in your mind, it presses downward into your soul causing you to seek the Good Shepard. This internal atmosphere enables hearing from God regardless of external events in our life. My favorite prayerful experiences have occurred when my prayer ended and I lingered by meditating on the goodness of God based upon scripture.

In that post prayer turned meditation time, God sometimes interrupts my thoughts to bring light to my soul. His voice is short, clear and to the point. His loving words are provided to encourage growth, but it also brings me closer to Him wanting more personal time. One such time, God interrupted my thoughts with a simple statement from the book of Revelations. He said "I have something against you". I responded with self-justification for a short time and I finally asked, Lord, what do you have against me? He responded that "you pass by people every day and that your hands are not dirty. You do not stop to look into their eyes and offer compassion." See, while I was living for God, He had more of Himself to place in me, that being a heart of a servant. I realized that I was just like the Priest and the Levite that passed by and didn't offer to help the person left for dead on the side of the road. I do help people in need, but God wanted me to seek helping others as a part of my daily life. I repented and made plans to travel my daily road as a servant and looked for ways I could minister in the community.

During my search I felt led to join Hospice as a volunteer. Despite being very tired in body, I was determined to get started, but before I could, I was diagnosed with leukemia. It was hard for me to stop, but truth be known I couldn't go any farther. During my treatment, the very fact that God had spoken to me and given me a calling, gave me faith to stand on. I quit praying for my healing and trusted God completely that I was going to be able to answer His call on my life.

This experience has encouraged me many times, but it is not the only time that I have heard God's voice. Once you wait upon Him and hear His voice, you will never forget it and will want more of Him. In this life, we are all on the road where bad things happen to people. Stop and get your hands dirty with compassion. Stoop and look into the eyes of the hurting. Read and meditate on His word, your prayers will have power simply because you are submissive and supportive of His love. The power of prayer reveals your inner depth in Christ. The last question I have for you is how deep do you want to go in Christ?

Cancer

During my hospital stay at Emory Hospital in Atlanta, Georgia, like most cancer patients, I had good and bad days. One day my wife, Lynn and I were talking of a good outcome for me and we started singing the chorus portion of an old song that says "I've got a feeling that everything is going to be alright". We sang that part over and over again and it lifted our spirits.

During one of my prayers, I was praising God for who He was and that he is an awesome God. I kept telling Him about how he was to me. When I got to the part in my prayer that I told Him the He was a no-matter-what God, he interrupted my thoughts and asked me if I would be a person of no-matter-what? It caught me off guard because I wasn't expecting the Holy Spirit to interrupt my prayer of praise. I stopped for a while to think about it mainly because I had not yet been cancer free yet. There were no guarantees for my health and future. After a short pause, I replied back to the Lord and said "Yes Lord, I will be a person of no matter what". Once I made that decision, I felt the peace that passes all understanding and soon after that I felt like I was living as described in the 23rd Psalms. I felt this way for a long time. I had many health problems after this point in time, but it never got me down because I had already made my decision to be a person of no-matter-what.

Gleaning

Reference: Leviticus 19:9-10 and Deuteronomy 24:19-21

As a child, my family was fortunate to partake in gleaning as outlined in the bible. The scriptures outline that the farmer should not completely harvest the fields leaving some for the poor, orphans, widows, and foreigners. The most famous story in the bible concerning gleaning is the story of Ruth gleaning in the field of Boaz in support of herself and mother-in-law. My Dad's sister, Leeta, lived near the potato farm fields in Michigan. We made preparations by buying large burlap sacks that would hold up to 100 pounds of potatoes if were fortunate enough to find that many potatoes.

Aunt Leeta would call my father and tell him where the farmers would be harvesting that Saturday. We would get up early and make the drive to the fields and wait for the farmer to give us permission to enter with directions as to where we could begin our search for potatoes. Dad, with his family in tow, would line up about six to ten feet apart and we began to probe the dirt on our hands and knees. We did this until we reached the other side of the field or until we had gathered enough potatoes to fill our burlap sacks. Us kids didn't mind the labor because we knew very well the stories of our parents growing up in the depression era. We made the best of it by announcing to the others that we had found a potato and we often made potato size comparisons.

Covered with dirt upon completing our mission, we brushed off as much dirt as we could using wet rags and towels. The dirt was especially stuck to our arms, legs and shoes. We and climbed into the car and made our way home. We were happy and very tired. We stored the potatoes in the basement which often had two to three inches of water on the floor. The little light the that came into the basement through a small window along with the moisture caused the potatoes that we had hung to sprout and grow more potatoes. I liked seeing them grow in the winter.

I believe that we gleaned for two years. On the third year, as we waited on the side of the field for the farmer's permission to enter the field, I remember the farmer telling my father that they weren't going to allow people into the fields anymore because someone had harvested potatoes ahead of the equipment. I watched my father's face flood with disappointment. He never said a thing; we all got back into the car and took the long silent trip back home. I have no doubt that my father wondered what we would do to make up the difference in groceries. I've seen this same type of thing occur in my life time-and-time again where some people cause others to lose the privilege because they couldn't respect others or the process.

I hope that people read this and are more considerate of their actions. With the gleaning principle in mind, life isn't all about them!

In Conclusion

For the longest time, I never gave the Holy Spirit much thought or credit, because I always thought about God and Jesus. Even though I felt led to take certain directions in my life when I prayed, I never made the connection it was the Holy Spirit guiding and moving me. In honesty, the Holy Spirit seemed to be another name associated with God and held little value to me personally. At times, I took Him for granted. At other times, you could go as far as to say I ignored Him altogether. Little did I know that He would be my key to overcoming myself and the problems I faced. It would be His testimony of Jesus that would prepare my heart to receive all the mercies, grace, and forgiveness that has led to my personal freedom and the renewal of my mind. It's one thing to be saved and still another to be saved and free. Having been both saved and saved with freedom, I can openly say the latter is not just a feeling but a superior way to live. I know I will have many more obstacles to overcome in life, as well as spiritually, because I have not yet arrived. But I have great comfort in the fact that I know His voice, and He knows mine.

In summary, this book is about the power of self-observation, confession, repentance, submission to the Lord and His word, and continual spiritual growth. I have reached the opinion that God wants each of us all to become disciples of the Lord, Jesus Christ. Lamentations 3:22-23, tells us that *"The steadfast love of the Lord never ceases; his mercies never come to an end; they are new every morning; great is your faithfulness"*. And because God demonstrates that His love is new every morning, we should also give attention daily to His direction to our lives and grow in His love and grace.

When the Lord first called me to write this book, I had no idea of all the things in my life that I would have to confront within myself, confess, repent of, and finally humble myself in order to place them into words on a page for everyone to see. It wasn't always easy to do, but I knew that it was what was required of me in order to demonstrate His character to each of us. Galatians 5:22-23, says that the fruit of the Holy Spirit is love, joy, peace, forbearance, kindness, goodness, faithfulness, gentleness, and self-control. The lord has shown each of these traits to me over my life time. They are given for us to develop as the very fabric of our character so that we might be Christ like. Just as God first gave His son, Jesus Christ, to die for our sins before we ever came into the knowledge of Him, God has also always demonstrated the fruit of the spirit towards us so that all might be saved and come into repentance of sins under Jesus Christ.

Now that this book is complete, I place it at the cross and ask Him to bless it for His namesake. The question I hope you seek an answer for is, "Does Jesus know me?" That is the real unit of measurement for our eternal security. If Jesus does know you, you should still take a moment of honest self-reflection and examine your standing with the Lord, Jesus Christ when compared with the Bible. Pray and seek the truth for yourself. No one can answer this question for you. Just like I stated in the poem "Returns", take a sounding to find your depth and location in Jesus Christ. You too can know the voice of the Holy Spirit so that your walk in Christ has both depth and assurance as you follow His leading. If you don't know Jesus as Lord and Savior, I am asking you to consider submitting your life to Jesus Christ. Pray Psalm 51:10 over yourself and ask for God to create in you a clean heart and to renew in me a right spirit within me. You will be blessed!

Thank you for reading this book. I pray that it helps you consider your ways and helps you to live intentionally for the Lord.

ABOUT THE AUTHORS

Steven Sieting

Graduating high school with very low reading and writing skills does not give you many options or much hope when you enter the workforce, so I knew college was not for me. I was as a young man wondering what to do with my life that caused me to seek God for direction. I felt impressed by Him to seek entry into the US Navy so I enlisted in 1976 as an Electronics Technician. I entered in 1976 in my chosen field of electronics. At the end of the yearlong school, I volunteered in large part because the pay was $75.00 more per month for the submarine service. I still work in the electronic field and enjoy working with engineer's designing, building, and repairing equipment. Engineers are fun to joke with because most of them are very detailed thinkers. I have overcome my learning disability by facing my embarrassment, not making excuses, and applying myself to the best of my ability.

I met my wife, Lynn, in California and proposed after four months. I loved her and felt led by the Lord to marry her. It was my goal to marry only once, and I am grateful for her. We have worked together to make a home where love matters. Lynn and I have been married for forty-four years, and together we have three children—Carey, Kevin, and Steven— and five grandsons. I love her more today than I ever have.

I know what it is like to know the Lord, fall away, and then try to find my way back to His presence. Having done so, I highly recommend you don't attempt it. It is not safe physically, spiritually, or mentally. I liken it to bungee jumping off the side of a mountain before you attach yourself to the cord. Don't do it! Some might consider me for the spiritual Darwin Awards, but I don't think I would be the only candidate for this award. I know joy and depression, laughter and sorrow, and I have come to the decision I am determined that, as in a marriage vow, I will love the Lord in sickness or in health, richer or poorer, and until death do I part.

God has your pathway covered if you place your faith in Him. As I stated in the begining of this book, that I felt led by the Lord to go into the navy. Although it was very hard on me because I was shy and I was not a good student, He walked and guided me through many difficult times giving me His reassurance that He loved me to much to let me go. I went from just passing each class to becoming very good in my field of work. After the navy, I applied for two jobs, and after that time, companies saught me to come and work for them. I interviewed them to concider if I wanted to work for them. I have been respected and worked in several engineering positions helping design, document and test new equipment. I've had a blessed career and enjoyed following my Lord and Savior.

Eleanor Sieting

The poetry written by my late mother, Eleanor Sieting, is included with the permission of my father, Milton Sieting. We knew she had written two poems, "Grieving" and "Despair," but after she died, I found a few more poem drafts. She did not give them titles, and for this book, I gave them titles as I saw fit. The poem "Grieving" is about my brother Richard who, near death due to encephalitis, caused my parents to be very distraught. As a very young child, I can still see my mother sitting on my father's lap as he held her in silence while she cried in the dark kitchen late one night. After fifty-two days in the hospital, Richard came home, where he still had a long recovery to endure.

Mother was the family communicator, and when she gave a direction, she had already thought it through, so there was little chance of changing her mind. She was tough, fair, and hardworking, and expected the same from each of her children. She did with as little as possible, so the family would have what it needed. When my parents were first married, Dad handled and spent every single cent. That changed when I pushed my sister into a bed while chasing her. Our neighbor, Mary, took us to the doctor's office and paid for the office visit. Mary gave my dad a very hard time about leaving his family without any money. They became the best of friends, and Mom took care of the money for the rest of her life. She never let him down, and when we were talking about her after her death,

Dad said she was one in a bazillion, and he would not have had anything if it wasn't for her. Dad was right.

My mother was very much a to-the-point person, so you did not have to wonder what she was thinking. She also had the saddest eyes I ever saw when one of her children disappointed her. Mom was very good with her hands and always making something. She turned mostly to tatting later in life, making crosses and giving them away to anyone she met. The last cross she gave away was when she entered the hospital for the last time. She started going in and out of dementia, and during a good time, she gave a cross to her nurse. The nurse broke down and cried. Turns out she was going through a divorce and needed a touch herself. Not long after this moment, my mother slipped away into dementia for her remaining time on earth. She had kept her promise to the Lord that she would make and give away crosses as long as He let her. So, I thought it was only fitting that the Lord let this be her final act.

Steven Sieting II

Steve Sieting II is my youngest son, and his poetry is entered into this book with his permission. The poems were written during his college years and given as gifts for Mother's and Father's Day presents to his mother and me. He is a graduate of Georgia Southern University. He lives in Warner Robins with his wife, Karin, and three boys. He spent his youth playing baseball on the local Little League fields and played through his high school years. I have watched him grow in the Lord as he tries to lead his family while being an overcomer.